EASY PIANO

CHART HITS OF 2019 2020

T0079500

ISBN 978-1-5400-8508-5

For all works contained herein:
Unauthorized copying, arranging, adapting, recording, Internet posting, public performance,
or other distribution of the music in this publication is an infringement of copyright.
Infringers are liable under the law.

Visit Hal Leonard Online at
www.halleonard.com

Contact us:
Hal Leonard
7777 West Bluemound Road
Milwaukee, WI 53213
Email: info@halleonard.com

In Europe, contact:
Hal Leonard Europe Limited
42 Wigmore Street
Marylebone, London, W1U 2RN
Email: info@halleonardeurope.com

In Australia, contact:
Hal Leonard Australia Pty. Ltd.
4 Lentara Court
Cheltenham, Victoria, 3192 Australia
Email: info@halleonard.com.au

ADORE YOU

Words and Music by HARRY STYLES,
THOMAS HULL, TYLER JOHNSON
and AMY ALLEN

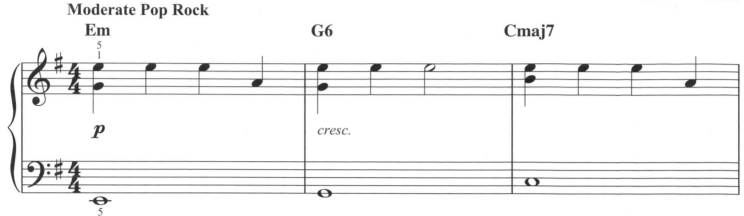

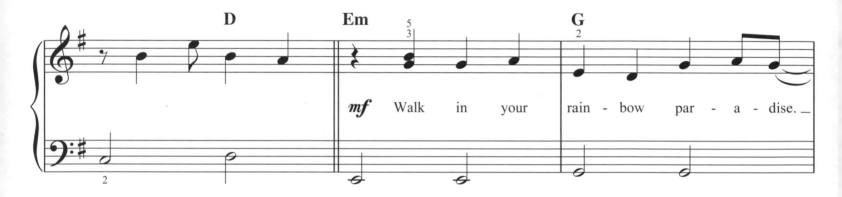

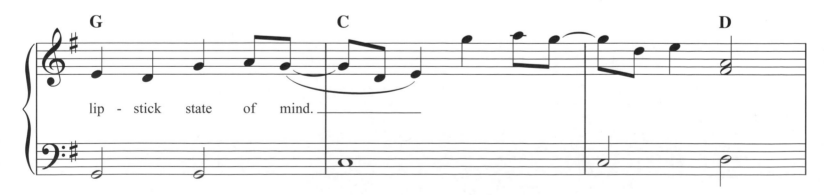

Copyright © 2019 UNIVERSAL MUSIC WORKS, HSA PUBLISHING LTD., UNIVERSAL MUSIC PUBLISHING LTD., THESE ARE PULSE SONGS,
ONE YEAR YESTERDAY PUBLISHING, CREATIVE PULSE MUSIC, SNAPPED BACK SONGS, KENNY + BETTY TUNES and ARTIST PUBLISHING GROUP WEST
All Rights for HSA PUBLISHING LTD. Administered by UNIVERSAL MUSIC WORKS
All Rights for UNIVERSAL MUSIC PUBLISHING LTD. in the United States and Canada Administered by UNIVERSAL - POLYGRAM INTERNATIONAL PUBLISHING, INC.
All Rights for ONE YEAR YESTERDAY PUBLISHING and CREATIVE PULSE MUSIC Administered by THESE ARE PULSE SONGS
All Rights for SNAPPED BACK SONGS, KENNY + BETTY TUNES and ARTIST PUBLISHING GROUP WEST Administered Worldwide by KOBALT SONGS MUSIC PUBLISHING
All Rights Reserved   Used by Permission

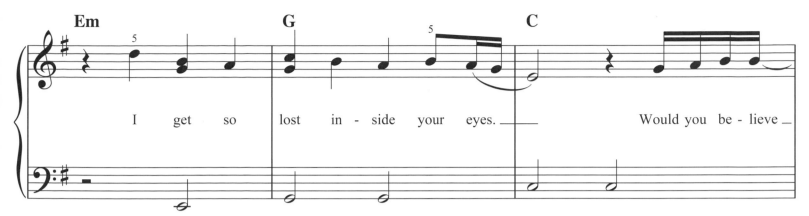

I get so lost in - side your eyes. Would you be - lieve _

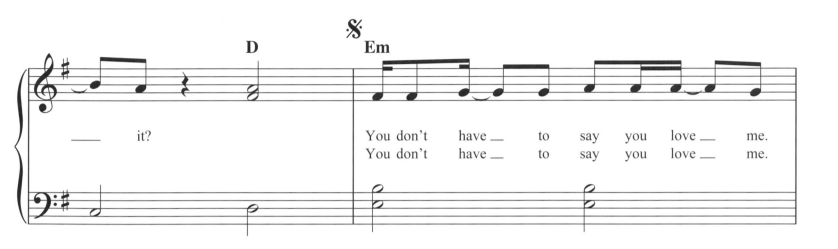

_ it?

You don't have _ to say you love _ me.
You don't have _ to say you love _ me.

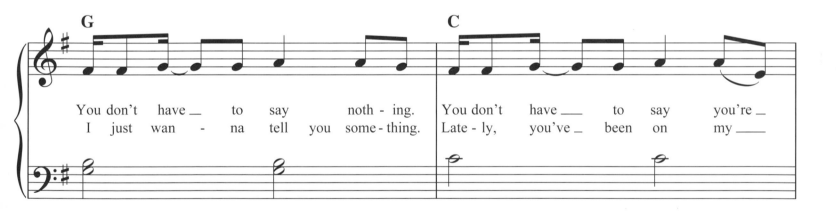

You don't have _ to say noth - ing. You don't have __ to say you're _
I just wan - na tell you some - thing. Late - ly, you've _ been on my ___

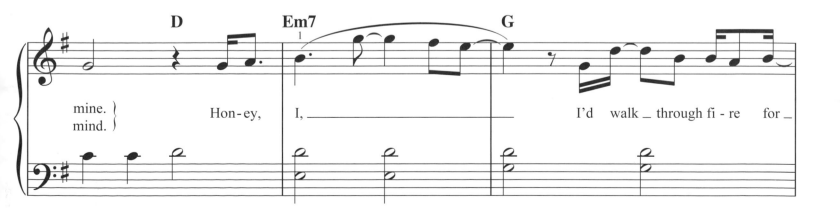

mine. } Hon - ey, I, ____ I'd walk _ through fi - re for _
mind. }

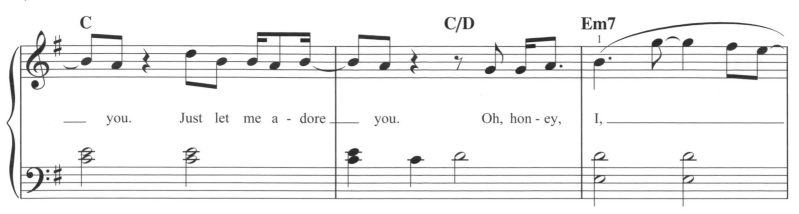

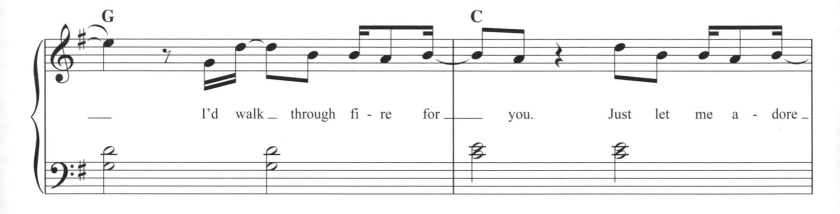

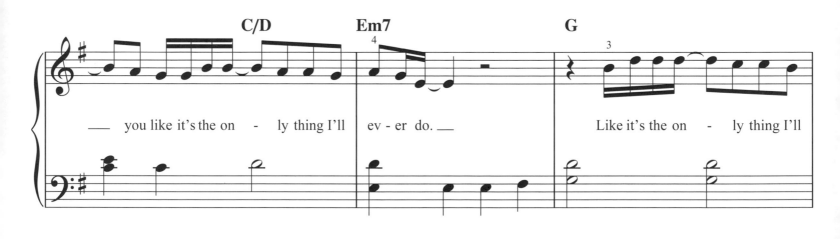

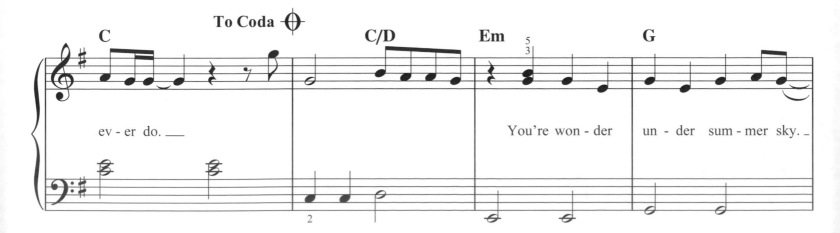

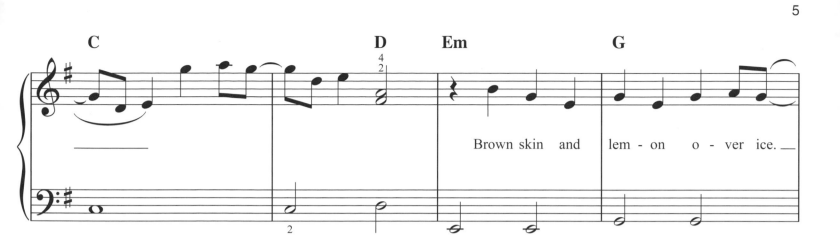

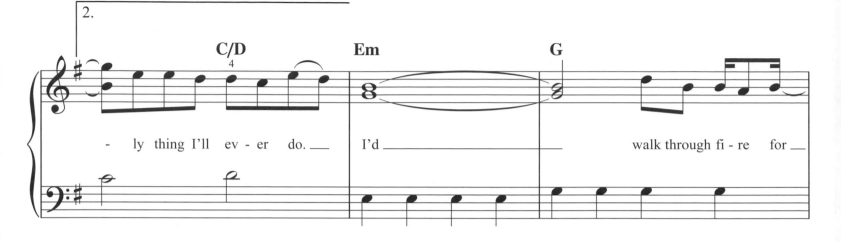

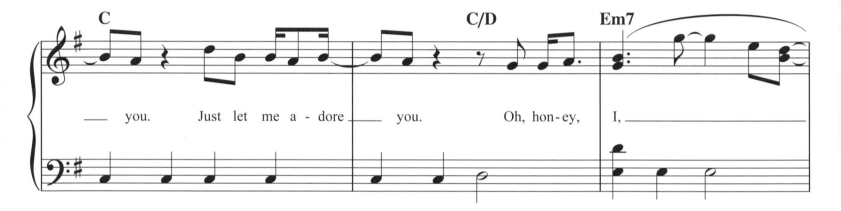

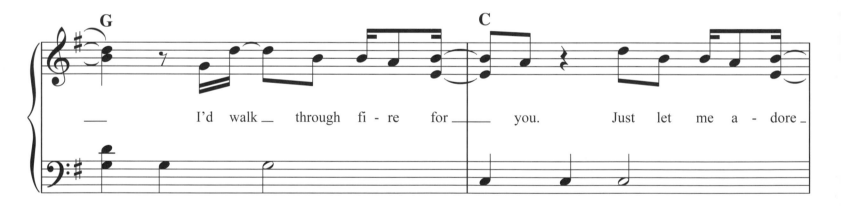

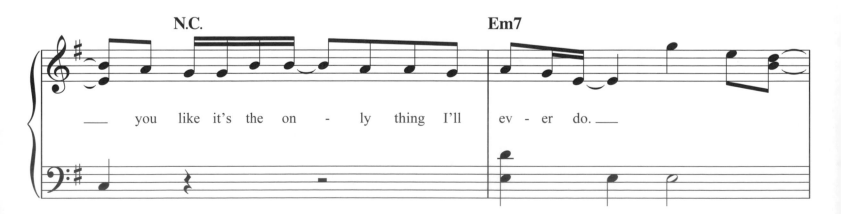

I'd walk _ through fi - re for _ you. Just let me a - dore _ you. Oh, hon - ey,

I, _____ I'd walk _ through fi - re for _ you. Just let me a - dore _

_ you. Oh, hon - ey.

Just let me a - dore _ you like it's the on - ly thing I'll ev - er do. _

BEAUTIFUL PEOPLE

Words and Music by ED SHEERAN,
KHALID ROBINSON, FRED GIBSON,
MAX MARTIN and SHELLBACK

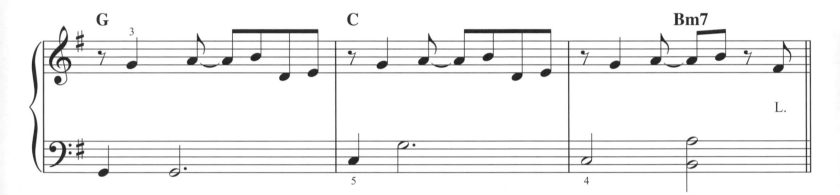

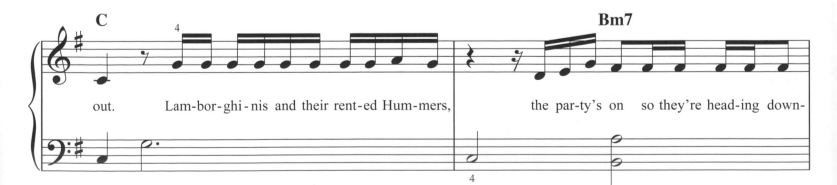

Copyright © 2019 Sony/ATV Music Publishing (UK) Limited, Sony/ATV Music Publishing LLC, Promised Land Music Ltd. and MXM
All Rights on behalf of Sony/ATV Music Publishing (UK) Limited and Sony/ATV Music Publishing LLC Administered by
Sony/ATV Music Publishing LLC, 424 Church Street, Suite 1200, Nashville, TN 37219
All Rights on behalf of Promised Land Music Ltd. Administered by Universal - PolyGram International Publishing, Inc.
All Rights on behalf of MXM Administered by Kobalt Songs Music Publishing
International Copyright Secured   All Rights Reserved

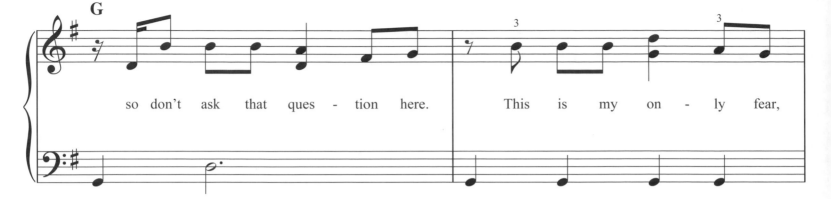

so don't ask that ques - tion here. This is my on - ly fear,

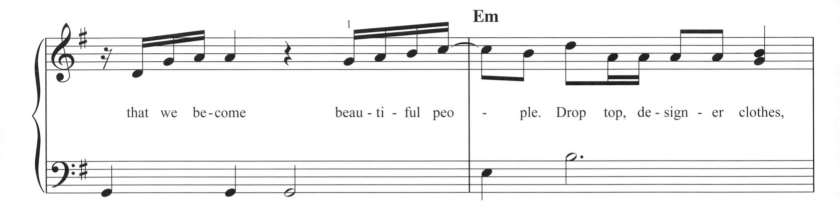

that we be - come beau - ti - ful peo - ple. Drop top, de - sign - er clothes,

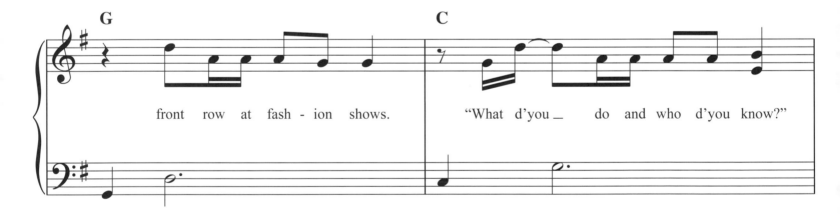

front row at fash - ion shows. "What d'you __ do and who d'you know?"

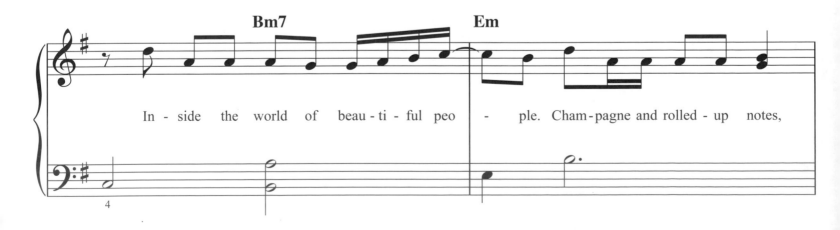

In - side the world of beau - ti - ful peo - ple. Cham - pagne and rolled - up notes,

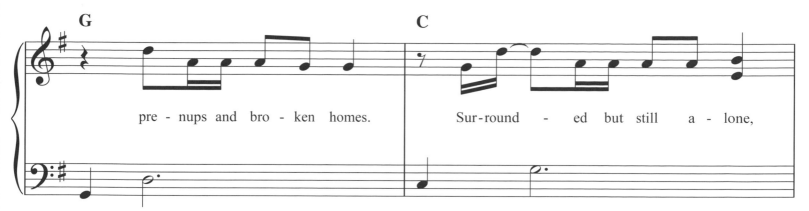

pre - nups and bro - ken homes.   Sur-round - ed but still a - lone,

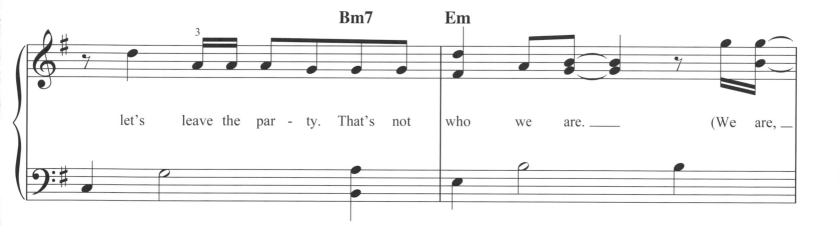

let's   leave the par - ty. That's not   who   we   are. _____   (We   are, _____

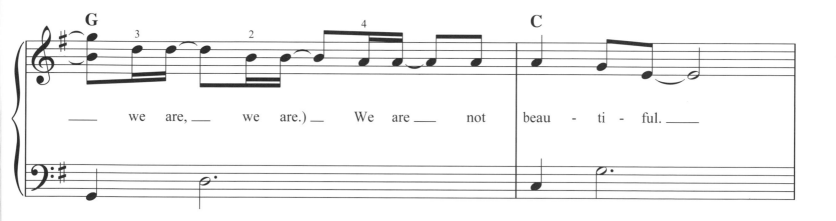

_____   we   are, _____   we   are.) _____   We   are _____   not   beau - ti - ful. _____

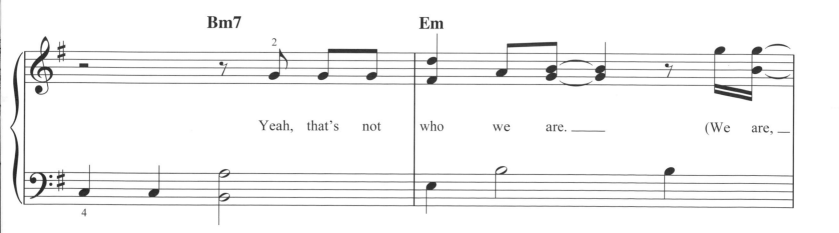

Yeah, that's   not   who   we   are. _____   (We   are, _____

cam - 'ras,   'cause with my   arms a - round __ you there's no need __ to

care. We   don't fit   in well

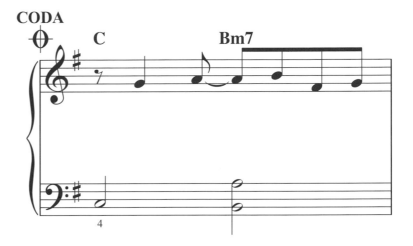

(We are, __   we are, __ we are.)   We are __ not

beau - ti - ful. __

BLINDING LIGHTS

Words and Music by ABEL TESFAYE,
MAX MARTIN, JASON QUENNEVILLE,
OSCAR HOLTER and AHMAD BALSHE

Fast dance beat

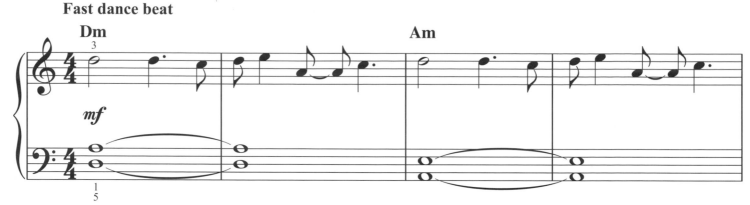

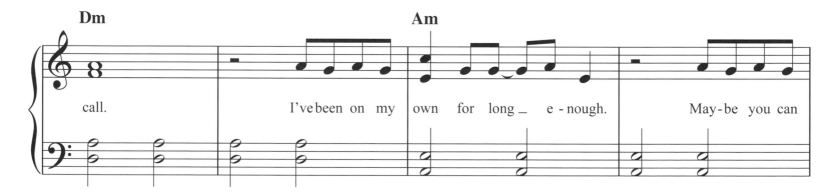

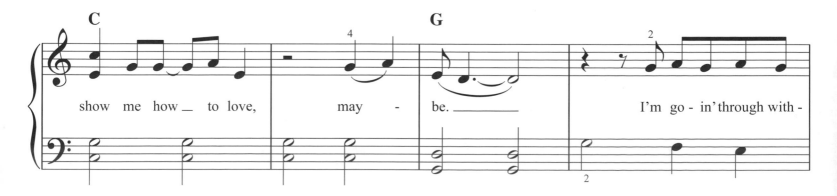

Copyright © 2019 KMR Music Royalties II SCSp, MXM, Universal Music Corp., Sal And Co LP, WC Music Corp. and Wolf Cousins
All Rights for KMR Music Royalties II SCSp and MXM Administered Worldwide by Kobalt Songs Music Publishing
All Rights for Sal And Co LP Administered by Universal Music Corp.
All Rights for Wolf Cousins Administered by WC Music Corp.
All Rights Reserved   Used by Permission

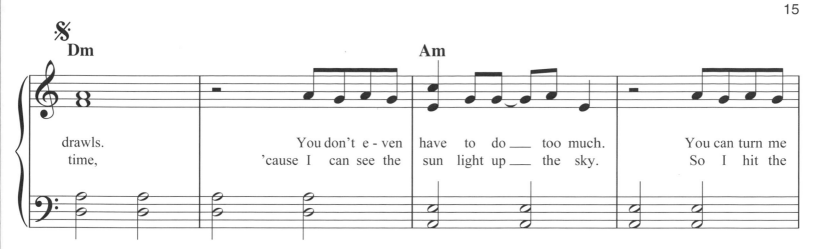

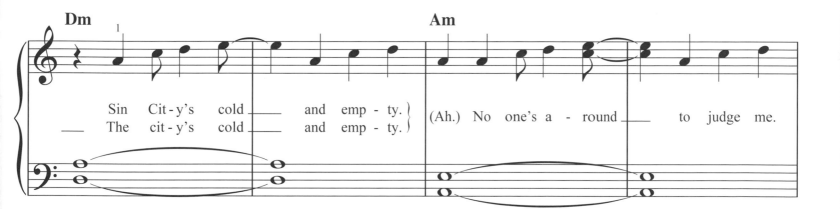

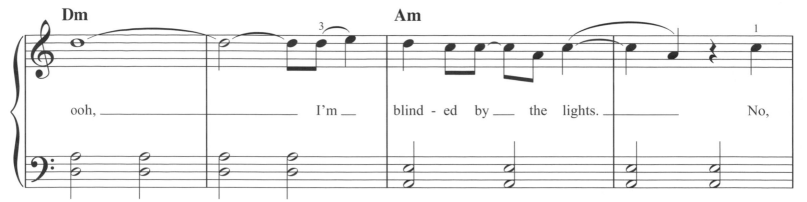

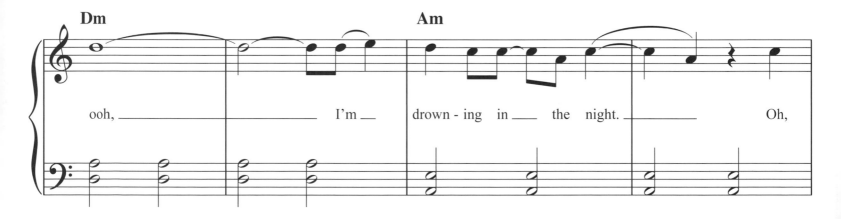

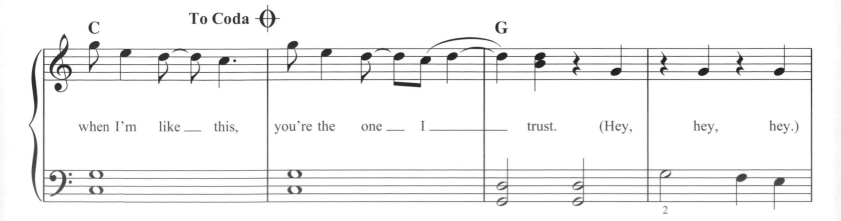

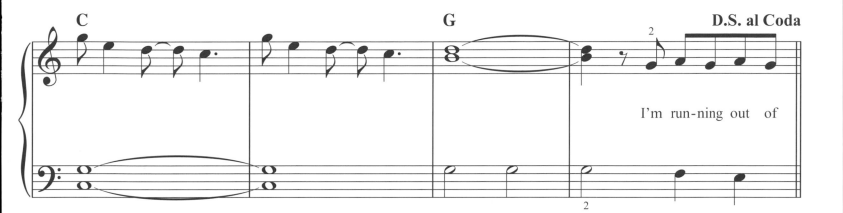

I'm run-ning out of

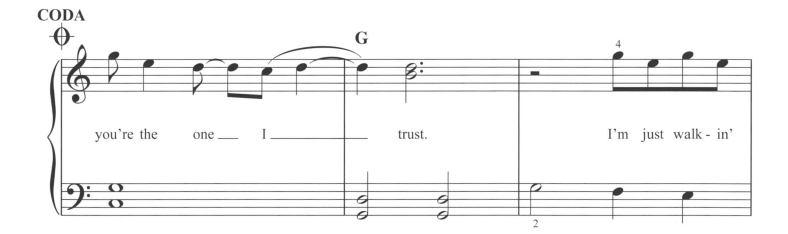

you're the one ___ I _____ trust.   I'm just walk - in'

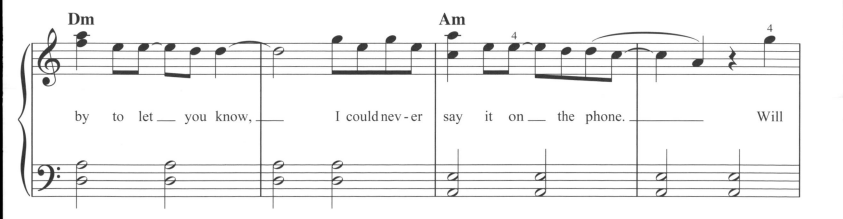

by to let ___ you know, ___   I could nev - er say it on ___ the phone. _____   Will

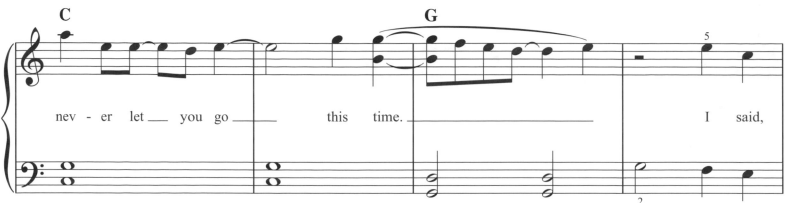

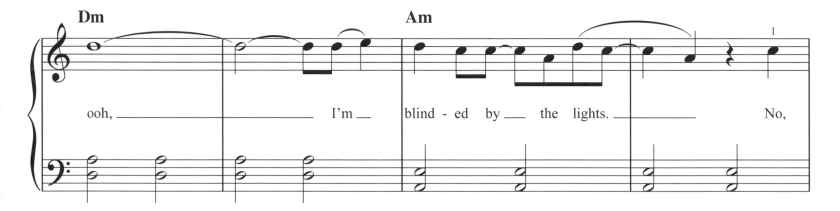

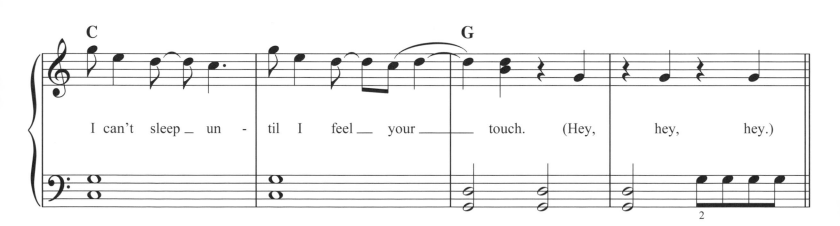

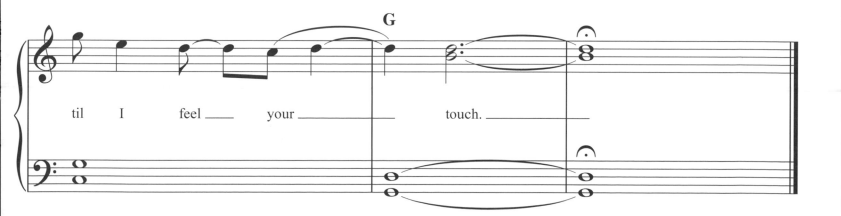

DON'T START NOW

Words and Music by DUA LIPA,
CAROLINE AILIN, IAN KIRKPATRICK
and EMILY SCHWARTZ

With energy

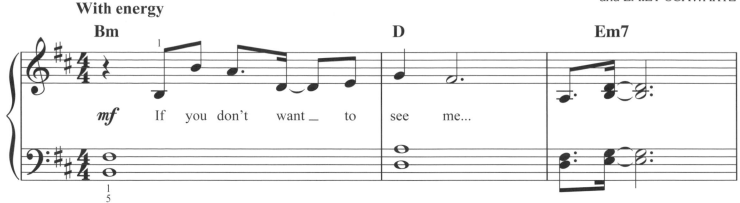

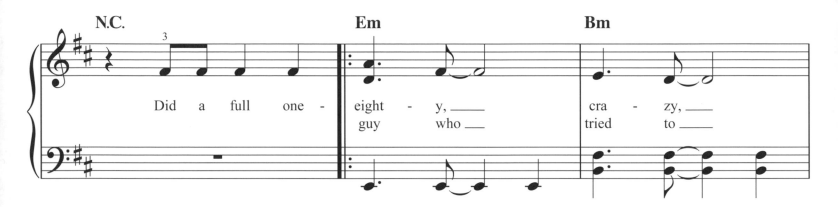

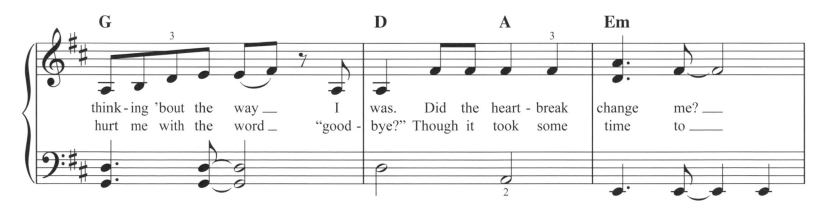

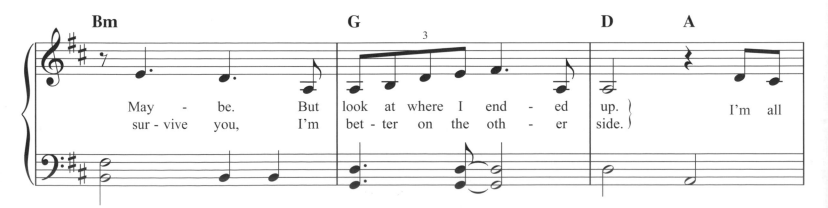

Copyright © 2019 TAP MUSIC PUBLISHING LTD., BMG RIGHTS MANAGEMENT SCANDINAVIA AB, WATERFALL MUSIC AS,
HAVENWOOD HOUSE, PRESCRIPTION SONGS, WARNER-TAMERLANE PUBLISHING CORP. and BUCKLEY TENENBAUM PUBLISHING
All Rights for TAP MUSIC PUBLISHING LTD. Administered by UNIVERSAL - POLYGRAM INTERNATIONAL PUBLISHING, INC.
All Rights for BMG RIGHTS MANAGEMENT SCANDINAVIA AB and WATERFALL MUSIC AS Administered by BMG RIGHTS MANAGEMENT (US) LLC
All Rights for HAVENWOOD HOUSE and PRESCRIPTION SONGS Administered Worldwide by KOBALT SONGS MUSIC PUBLISHING
All Rights for BUCKLEY TENENBAUM PUBLISHING Administered by WARNER-TAMERLANE PUBLISHING CORP.
All Rights Reserved   Used by Permission

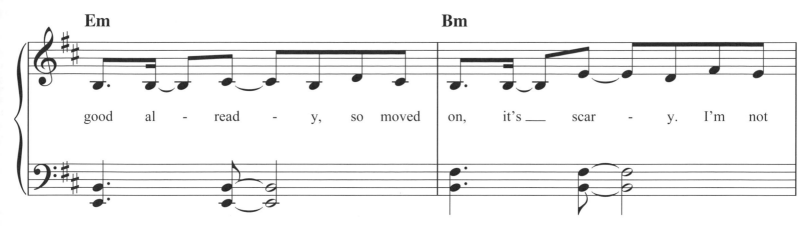

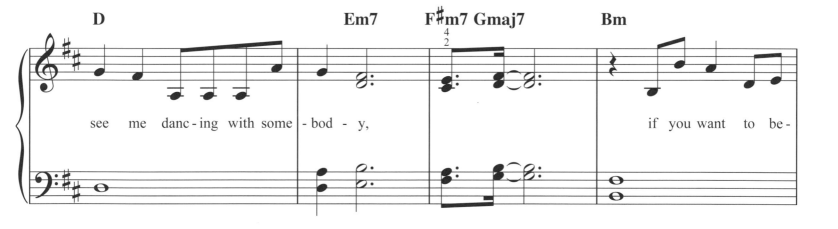

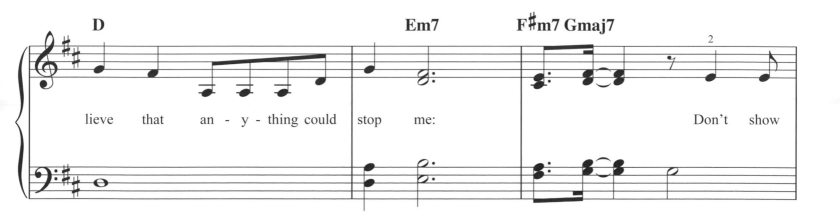

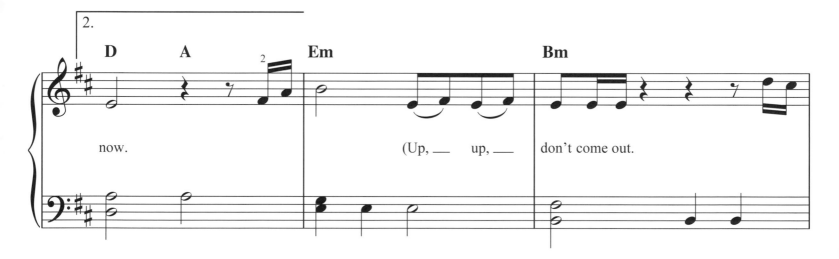

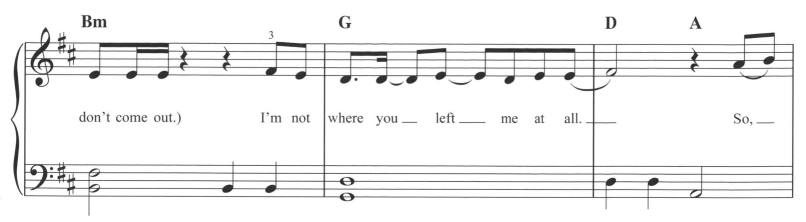

don't come out.) I'm not where you __ left __ me at all. __ So, __

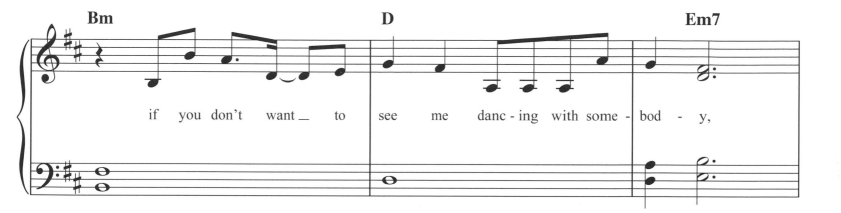

if you don't want __ to see me danc - ing with some - bod - y,

if you want to be - lieve that an - y - thing could

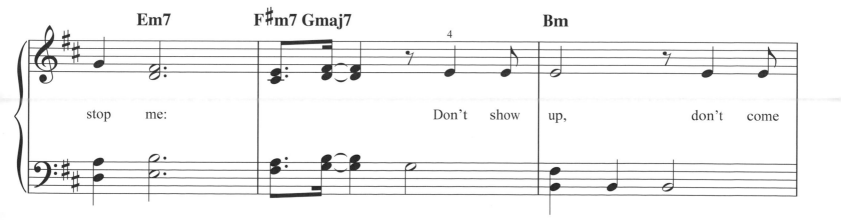

stop me: Don't show up, don't come

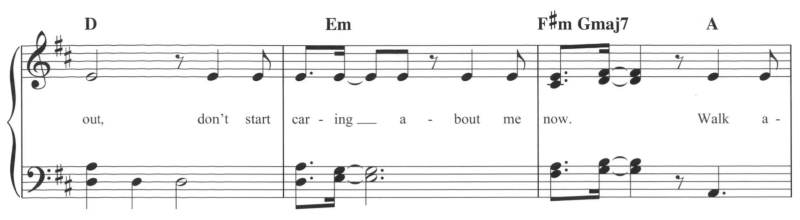

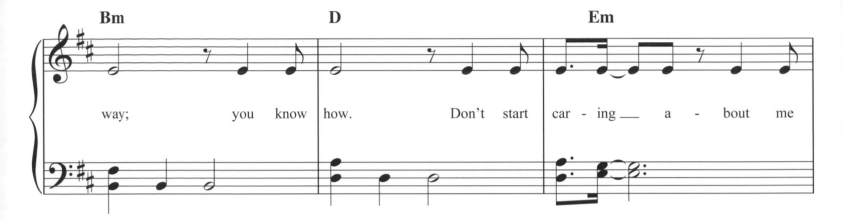

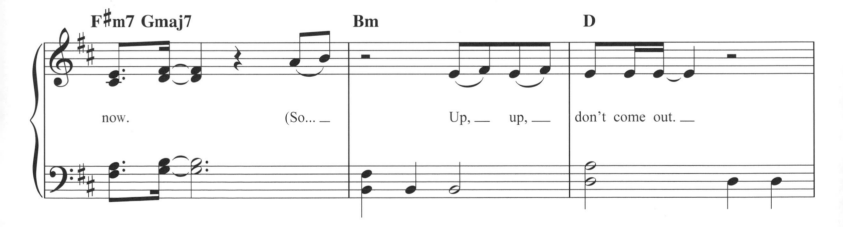

CIRCLES

Words and Music by AUSTIN POST,
KAAN GUNESBERK, LOUIS BELL,
WILLIAM WALSH and ADAM FEENEY

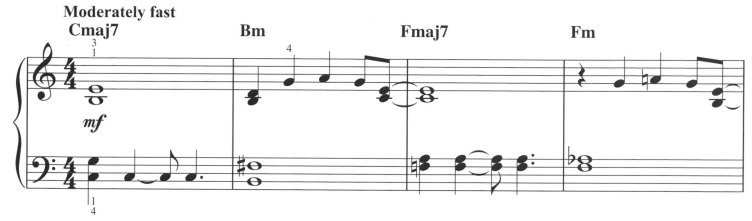

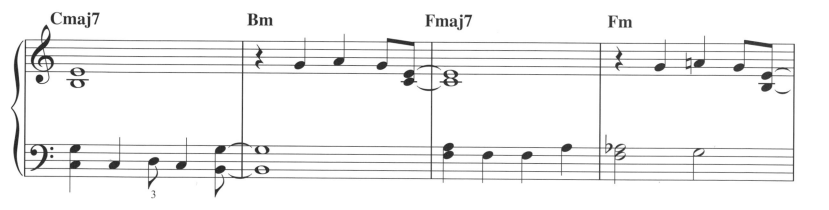

Copyright © 2019 SONGS OF UNIVERSAL, INC., POSTY PUBLISHING, UNIVERSAL MUSIC CORP.,
EMI APRIL MUSIC INC., NYANKINGMUSIC, WMMW PUBLISHING and ADAM FEENEY PUBLISHING DESIGNEE
All Rights for POSTY PUBLISHING Administered by SONGS OF UNIVERSAL, INC.
All Rights for EMI APRIL MUSIC INC., NYANKINGMUSIC and WMMW PUBLISHING Administered by
SONY/ATV MUSIC PUBLISHING LLC, 424 Church Street, Suite 1200, Nashville, TN 37219
All Rights Reserved   Used by Permission

We could-n't turn a - round

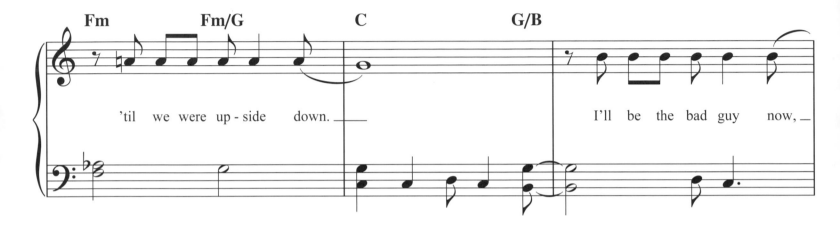

'til we were up-side down. I'll be the bad guy now,

but no, I ain't too proud.

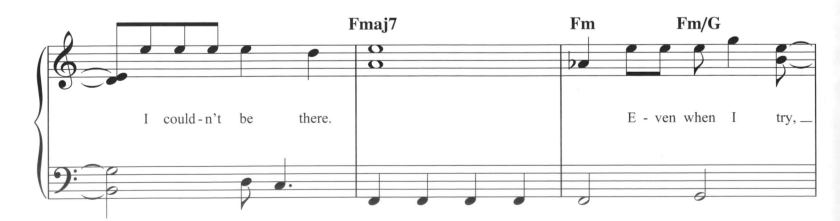

I could-n't be there. E - ven when I try,

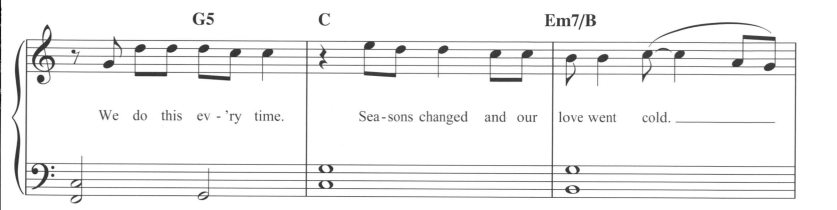

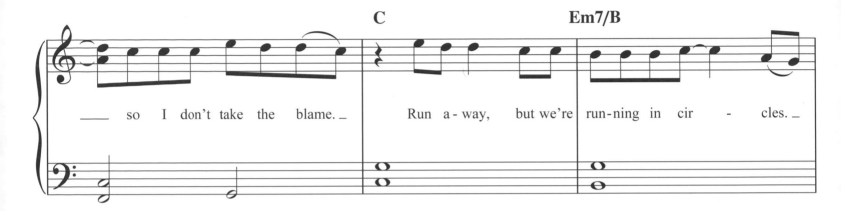

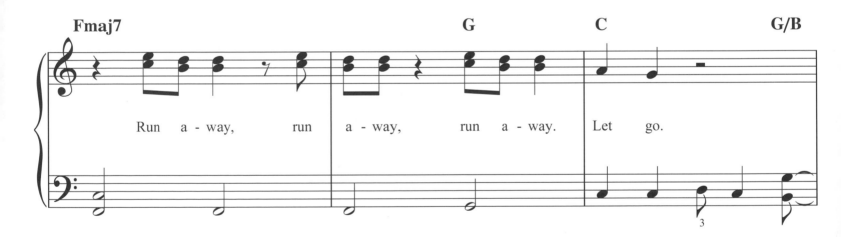

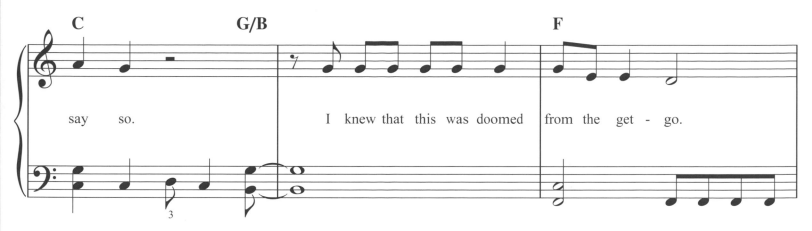

say so.   I knew that this was doomed | from the get - go.

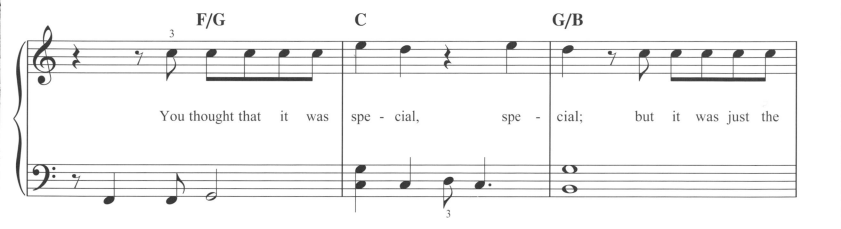

You thought that   it   was | spe - cial,   spe - | cial;   but   it   was just the

sex,   oh,   the   sex, | though.   And   I   still hear the | ech - oes,   the ech -

oes. I   got   a   feel - ing that it's | time   to   let   it   go. | Let   it   go.

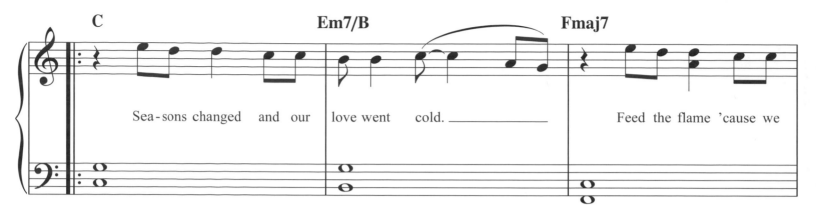

Sea-sons changed and our love went cold. _____ Feed the flame 'cause we

can't let go. _____ Run a - way, but we're run-ning in cir - cles. __

Run a - way, run a - way. I dare you to do ___ some - thing.

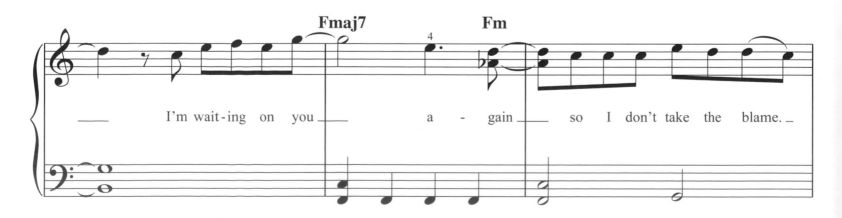

___ I'm wait-ing on you ___ a - gain ___ so I don't take the blame. __

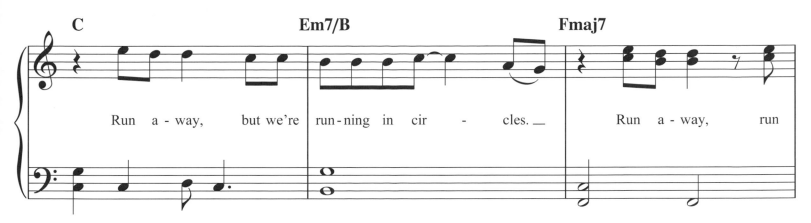

Run a-way, but we're run-ning in cir - cles. Run a-way, run

a - way, run a - way. May-be you don't un - der - stand what I'm go - ing through.

It's on - ly me; what you got to lose? Make up your mind. Tell me,

what are you gon - na do? It's on - ly me. Let it go.

DANCE MONKEY

Words and Music by
TONI WATSON

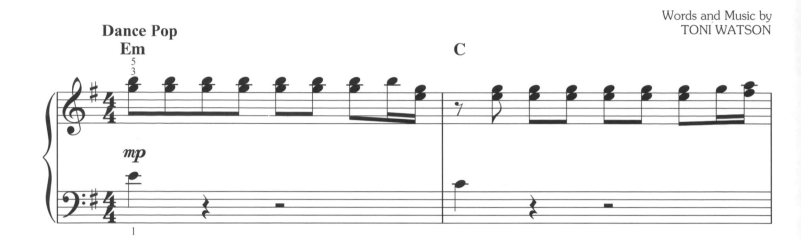

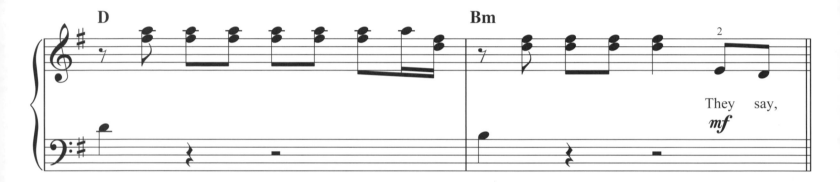

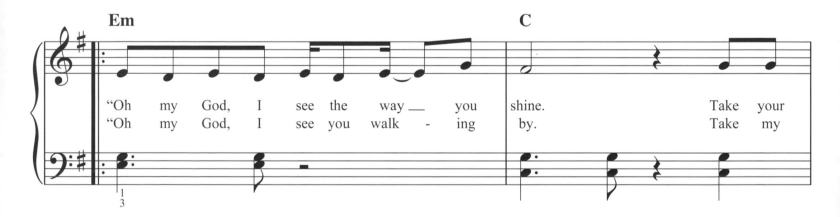

"Oh my God, I see the way __ you shine. Take your
"Oh my God, I see you walk - ing by. Take my

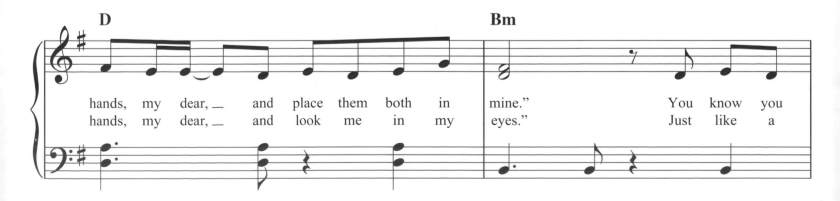

hands, my dear, __ and place them both in mine." You know you
hands, my dear, __ and look me in my eyes." Just like a

© 2019 TONE AND I PUBLISHING
All Rights Administered by WARNER-TAMERLANE PUBLISHING CORP.
All Rights Reserved   Used by Permission

34

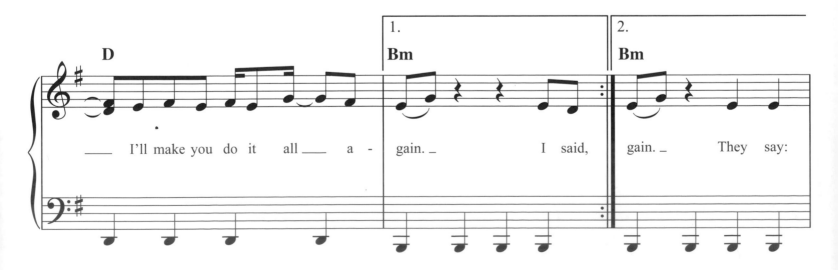

Dance for me, dance for me, dance for me, oh, oh, ___ oh, oh, oh, oh. I've nev - er seen ___

___ an - y - bod - y do the ___ things you do be - fore. ___ They say:

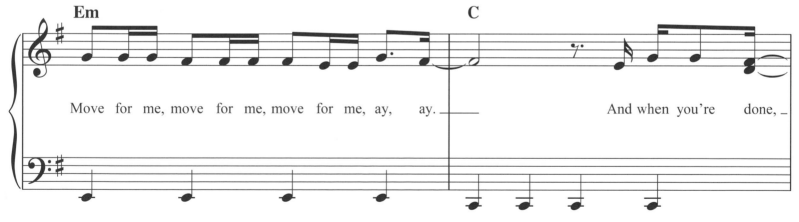

Move for me, move for me, move for me, ay, ay. ___ And when you're done, _

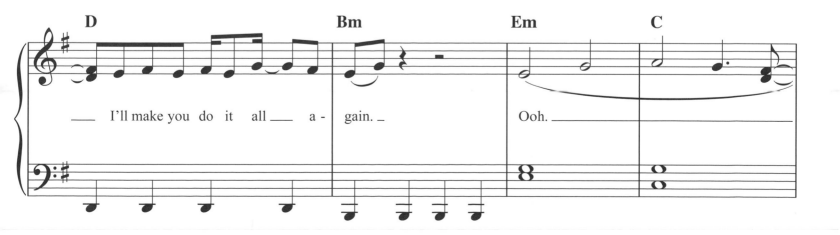

___ I'll make you do it all ___ a - gain. _ Ooh. ___

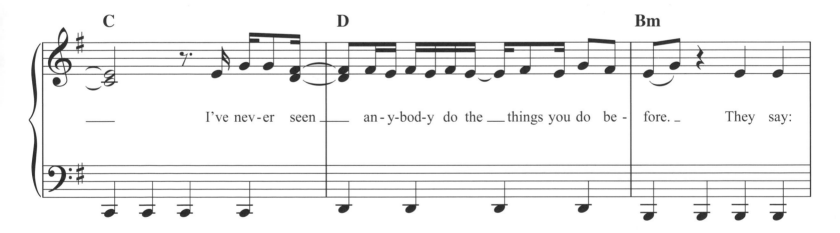

_____ I'll make you do it all _____ a - gain. _____ They say: Dance for me, dance for me, dance for me, oh, oh, _____

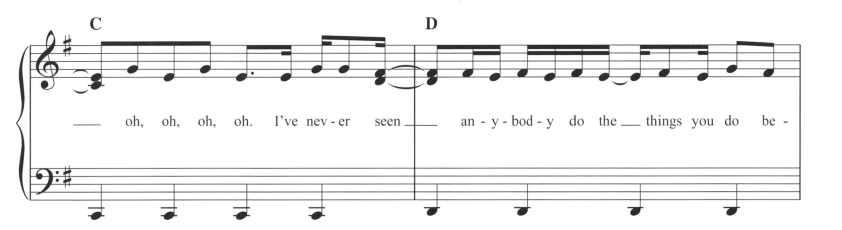

_____ oh, oh, oh, oh. I've nev - er seen _____ an - y - bod - y do the _____ things you do be -

fore. _____ They say: Move for me, move for me, move for me, ay, ay. _____ And when you're done, _____

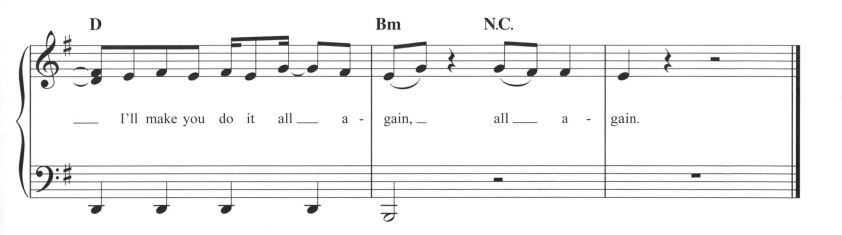

_____ I'll make you do it all _____ a - gain, _____ all _____ a - gain.

EVERYTHING I WANTED

Words and Music by BILLIE EILISH O'CONNELL
and FINNEAS O'CONNELL

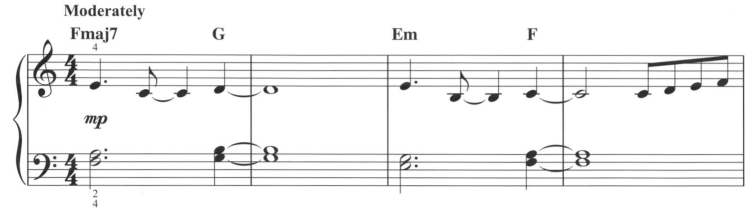

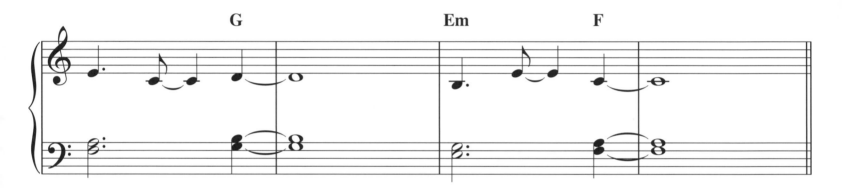

I had a dream   I got ev - 'ry - thing I

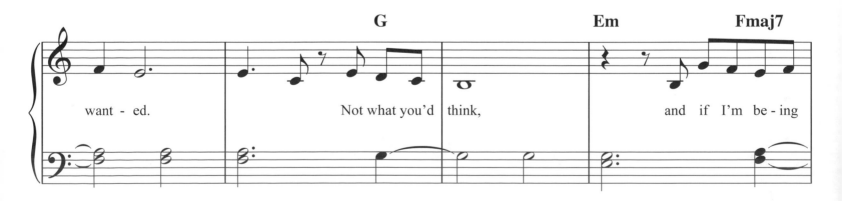

want - ed.   Not what you'd think,   and if I'm be - ing

Copyright © 2019 UNIVERSAL MUSIC CORP., DRUP and LAST FRONTIER
All Rights for DRUP Administered by UNIVERSAL MUSIC CORP.
All Rights for LAST FRONTIER Administered Worldwide by KOBALT SONGS MUSIC PUBLISHING
All Rights Reserved   Used by Permission

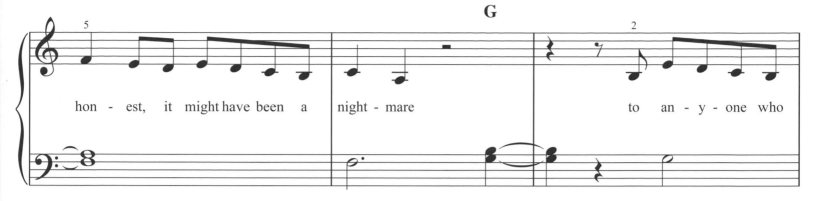

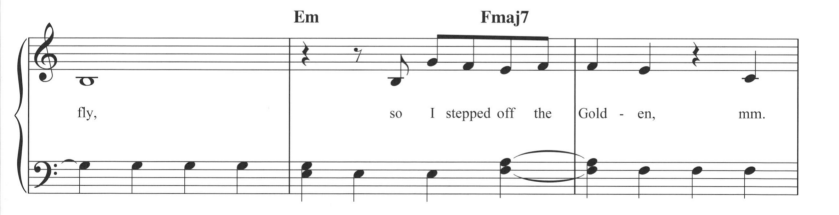

no - ticed. I saw them stand-ing right there, kind - a thought they

might care. I had a

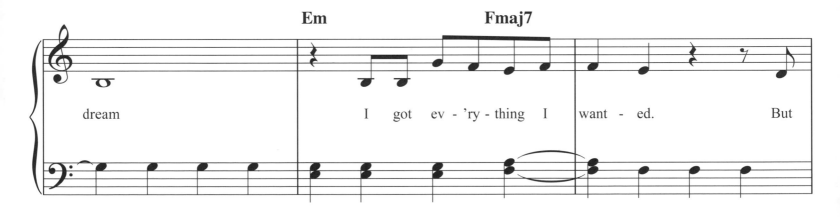

dream I got ev - 'ry-thing I want - ed. But

when I wake up, I see you with ___ me. ___

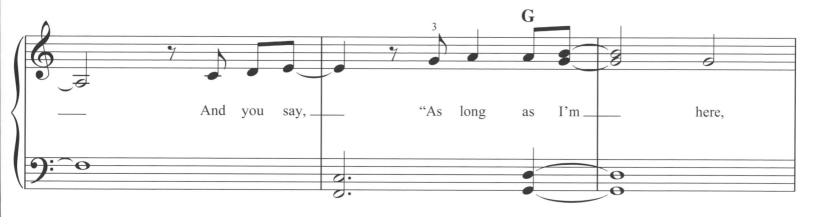

And you say, "As long as I'm here,

no one can hurt you. Don't want to lie here,

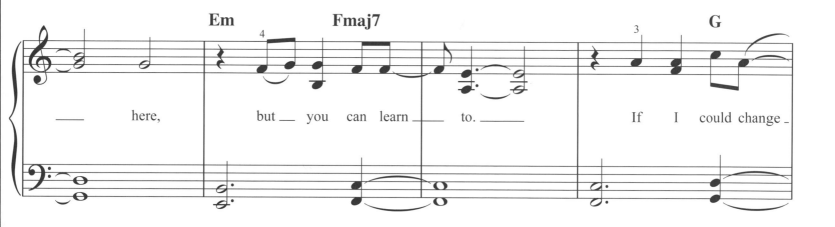

but you can learn to. If I could change

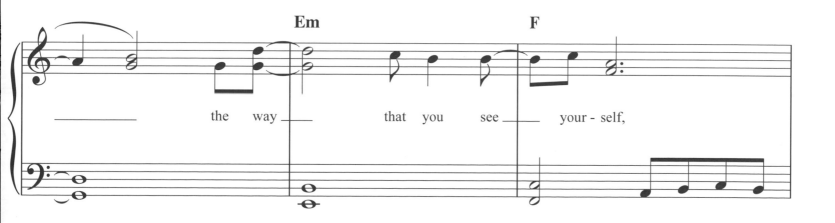

the way that you see yourself,

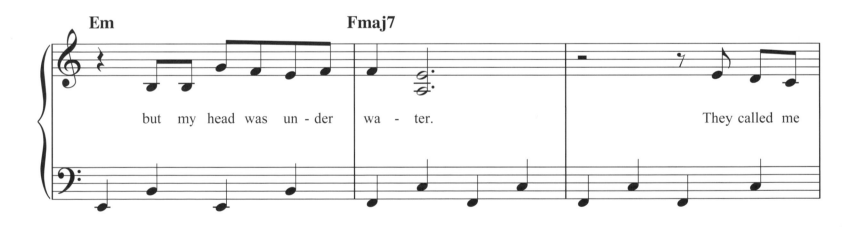

night - mare,   but it felt like they were   right   there.

And it   feels like yes - ter - day   was   a   year a - go,   but

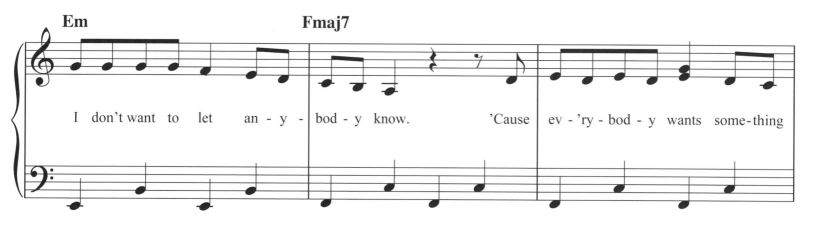

I don't want to let an - y - bod - y know.   'Cause ev - 'ry - bod - y wants some - thing

from me now,   and   I don't want to let them down.

44

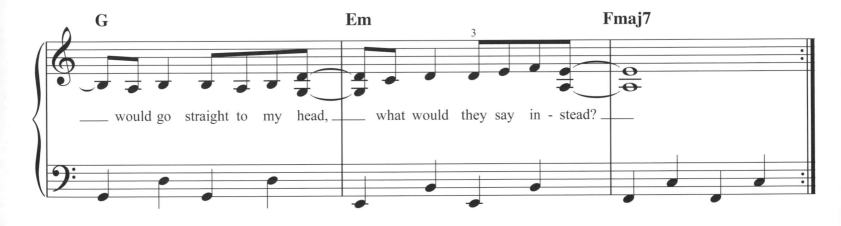

GOOD AS HELL

Words and Music by LIZZO
and ERIC FREDERIC

I do my hair toss, check my nails. __ Ba - by, how you feel - ing? (Feel - ing good as hell.) __

Hair toss, check my nails. __ Ba - by, how you feel - ing? (Feel - ing good as hell.) __

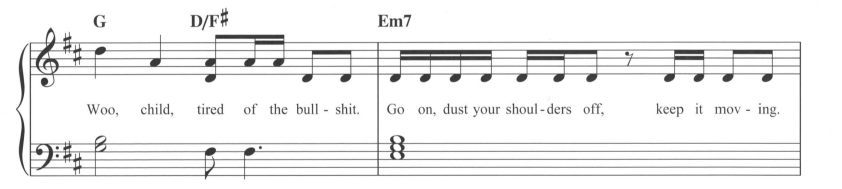

Woo, child, tired of the bull - shit. Go on, dust your shoul - ders off, keep it mov - ing.

Yes, Lord, tryin' to get some new shit, in there, swim - wear, go - ing to the pool shit.

© 2016 WARNER-TAMERLANE PUBLISHING CORP., MELISSA JEFFERSON PUBLISHING DESIGNEE,
SONY/ATV MUSIC PUBLISHING LLC, SONGS FROM THE BOARDWALK and FREDERIC AND RIED MUSIC
All Rights for MELISSA JEFFERSON PUBLISHING DESIGNEE Administered by WARNER-TAMERLANE PUBLISHING CORP.
All Rights for SONY/ATV MUSIC PUBLISHING LLC, SONGS FROM THE BOARDWALK and FREDERIC AND RIED MUSIC Administered by
SONY/ATV MUSIC PUBLISHING LLC, 424 Church Street, Suite 1200, Nashville, TN 37219
All Rights Reserved   Used by Permission

Come now, come dry your eyes. _ You know you're a star, you can touch the sky. _ I know that it's
Boss up and change your life. _ You can have it all, no _ sac - ri - fice. _ I know he did you

hard, but you have to try. _ If you need ad - vice, let me sim - pli - fy. _ If
wrong; we can make it right, _ so go and let it all hang _ out to - night. _ 'Cause

he don't love you an - y - more, _ just walk your fine ass out the door. _ I do my
he don't love you an - y - more, _ so walk your fine ass out the door _ and do your

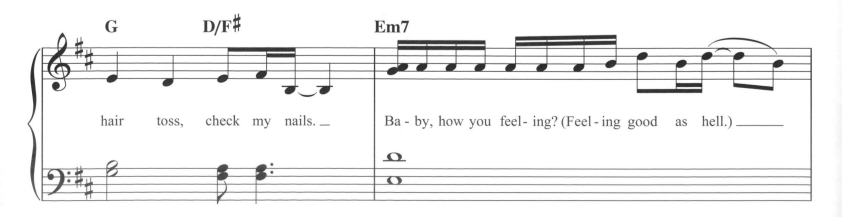

hair toss, check my nails. _ Ba - by, how you feel - ing? (Feel - ing good as hell.) _

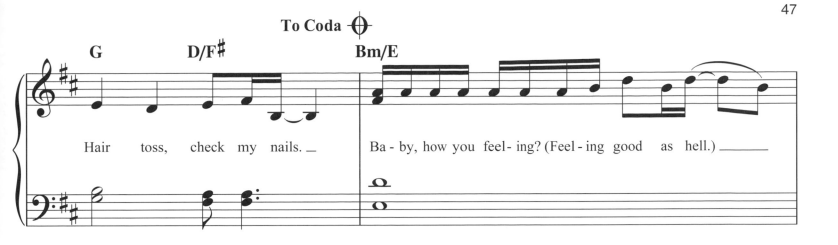

Hair toss, check my nails. __ Ba - by, how you feel- ing? (Feel- ing good as hell.) _____

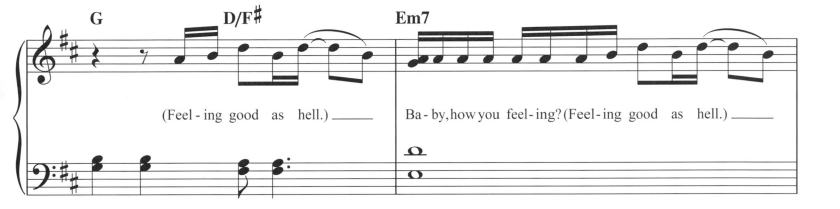

(Feel - ing good as hell.) _____ Ba - by, how you feel- ing? (Feel- ing good as hell.) _____

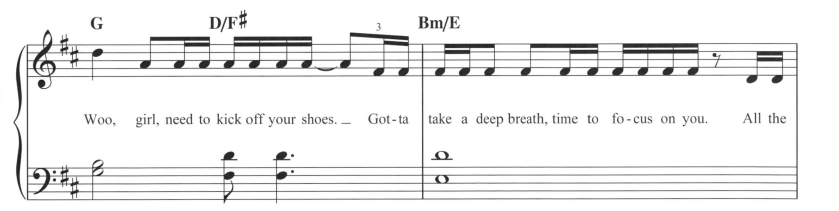

Woo, girl, need to kick off your shoes. __ Got- ta take a deep breath, time to fo - cus on you. All the

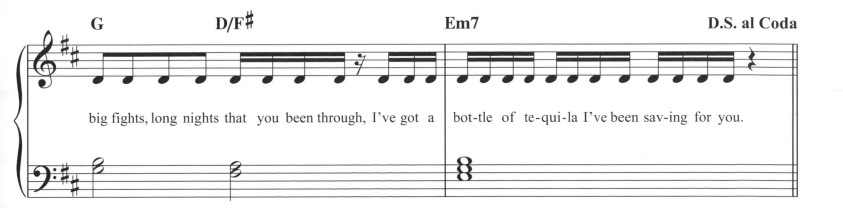

big fights, long nights that you been through, I've got a bot- tle of te- qui- la I've been sav- ing for you.

CODA

Ba - by, how you feel - ing? (Feel - ing good as hell.) _____ Hair toss, check my nails. _

Ba - by, how you feel - ing? (Feel - ing good as hell.) _____ Hair toss, check my nails. _

Ba - by, how you feel - ing? (Feel - ing good as hell.) _____ Hmm, _

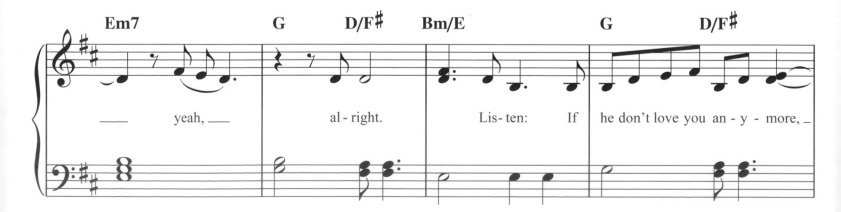

_____ yeah, _____ al - right. Lis - ten: If he don't love you an - y - more, _

then walk your fine ass out the door.

And do your

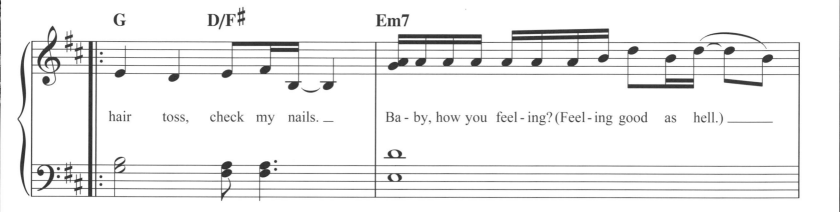

hair toss, check my nails. _

Ba - by, how you feel - ing? (Feel - ing good as hell.) _____

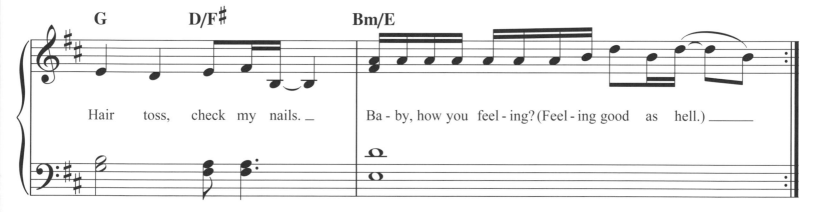

Hair toss, check my nails. _

Ba - by, how you feel - ing? (Feel - ing good as hell.) _____

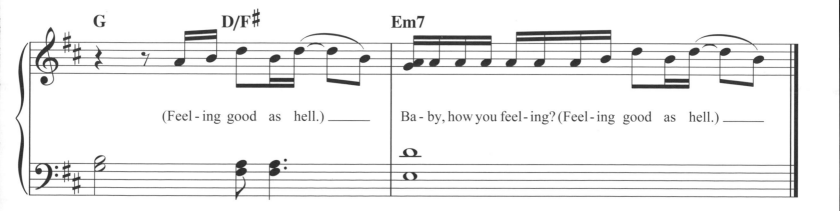

(Feel - ing good as hell.) _____

Ba - by, how you feel - ing? (Feel - ing good as hell.) _____

GOODBYES

Words and Music by AUSTIN POST,
BRIAN LEE, LOUIS BELL, WILLIAM WALSH,
JEFFREY LAMAR WILLIAMS, VAL BLAVATNIK
and JESSIE LAUREN FOUTZ

Moderately slow

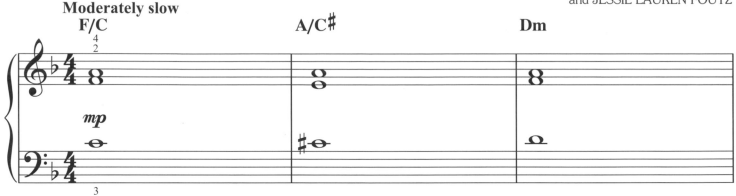

Me and Kurt feel the same; too much pleas-ure is pain.

My girl spites me in vain, all I do is com-plain,

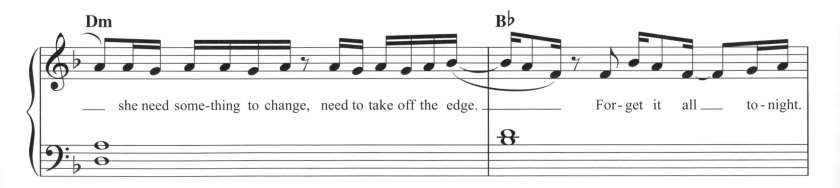

she need some-thing to change, need to take off the edge. For-get it all to-night.

Copyright © 2019 SONGS OF UNIVERSAL, INC., POSTY PUBLISHING, DONG HOE MUSIC, EMI APRIL MUSIC INC., NYANKINGMUSIC, WMMW PUBLISHING, RESERVOIR 416,
YOUNG STONER LIFE PUBLISHING, WARNER-TAMERLANE PUBLISHING CORP., VALENTIN BLAVATNIK PUB DESIGNEE and JESSIE LAUREN FOUTZ PUBLISHING DESIGNEE
All Rights for POSTY PUBLISHING and DONG HOE MUSIC Administered by SONGS OF UNIVERSAL, INC.
All Rights for EMI APRIL MUSIC INC., NYANKINGMUSIC and WMMW PUBLISHING Administered by
SONY/ATV MUSIC PUBLISHING LLC, 424 Church Street, Suite 1200, Nashville, TN 37219
All Rights for RESERVOIR 416 and YOUNG STONER LIFE PUBLISHING Administered Worldwide by RESERVOIR MEDIA MANAGEMENT, INC.
All Rights for VALENTIN BLAVATNIK PUB DESIGNEE Administered by WARNER-TAMERLANE PUBLISHING CORP.
All Rights Reserved   Used by Permission

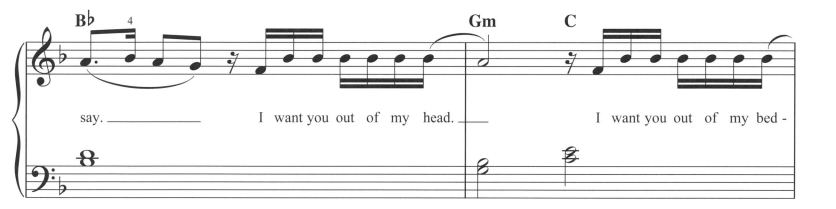

Now I'm drink-ing a-gain, eight-y proof in my veins. And my fin-ger-tips stained, look-ing o-ver the

edge. Don't mess with me to-night. Said you need-ed this heart and you got it.

Turns out that it was-n't what you want-ed. And we would-n't let go and we lost it.

Now I'm a gon-er. I want you out of my head. I want you out of my bed-

Am **Dm** **Bb**

- room to-night. There's no way I can save _____ you 'cause I need to be saved, __

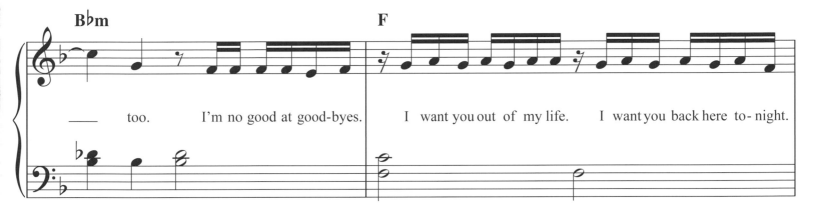

Bbm **F**

__ too. I'm no good at good-byes. I want you out of my life. I want you back here to-night.

A **Dm**

I'm try'n' to cut you, no knife. I wan-na slice you and dice you. My ar-gue pos-ses - sive, it got you pre-cise. _

Bb **F**

__ Can you not turn off the T-V? I'm watch-ing the fight. I flood the gar-age, __ blue dia-mond, no shark. _

Your Bar-bie life doll, _____ it's Nick-i Mi- naj. You don't need a key to drive; your car on the charg-

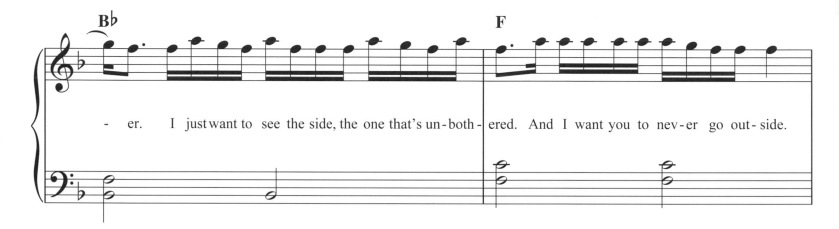

- er.   I just want to see the side, the one that's un-both- ered. And I want you to nev-er go out- side.

I prom-ise if they play, my slid-ing, slid-ing.   I'm with _ her and the tour bus still rid - ing.

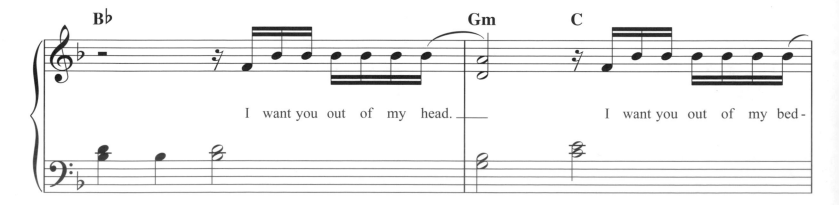

I want you out of my head. ____   I want you out of my bed-

- room to-night. There's no way I can save ___ you 'cause I need to be saved, __

___ too. I'm no good at good-byes. ___ Good-bye, __ good-bye, __ good-bye. __

___ Good-bye, __ good-bye, __ good-bye. ___ Good-bye, __ good-bye, __ good-bye. __

___ I'm no good at good-byes. ___

HEY LOOK MA, I MADE IT

Words and Music by BRENDON URIE,
DILLON FRANCIS, SAMUEL HOLLANDER,
MICHAEL ANGELAKOS, JACOB SINCLAIR
and MORGAN KIBBY

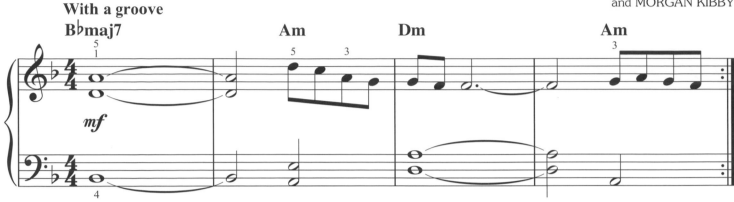

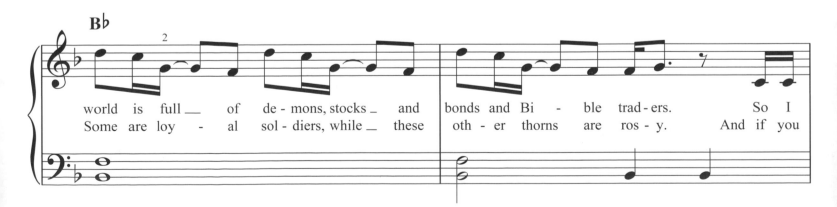

Copyright © 2018 Listen To This Shhh, Elephant Squirrel Publishing, 12th And Spring Garden, Prescription Songs, Hipgnosis Songs Fund Limited,
Songs Of Universal, Inc., Boat Builder Music Publishing LLC, Big Deal Beats, Sinclair Empire and Morgan Grace Music
All Rights for Listen To This Shhh, Elephant Squirrel Publishing, 12th And Spring Garden, Prescription Songs
and Hipgnosis Songs Fund Limited Administered Worldwide by Kobalt Songs Music Publishing
All Rights for Boat Builder Music Publishing LLC Administered by Songs Of Universal, Inc.
All Rights for Big Deal Beats and Sinclair Empire Administered by Words & Music
All Rights Reserved   Used by Permission

Dm

do the deed, __ get up and leave, __ a climb - er and __ a sa - dist, yeah. __
nev - er know __ who you can trust, __ then trust me, you'll __ be lone - ly, oh. __

B♭

Are you read - y for the se - quel?

Am

Ain't read - y for the lat - est?

Dm

In the gar - den of e - vil,

F

I'm gon - na be the great - est.

B♭

In a gold - en ca - the - dral.

Am

I'll be pray - ing for the faith - less. __ And

if you lose, boo - hoo. Hey, look, Ma, I made it. Hey, look Ma, I

made it. Ev-'ry-thing's com-ing up ac - es, ac - es.

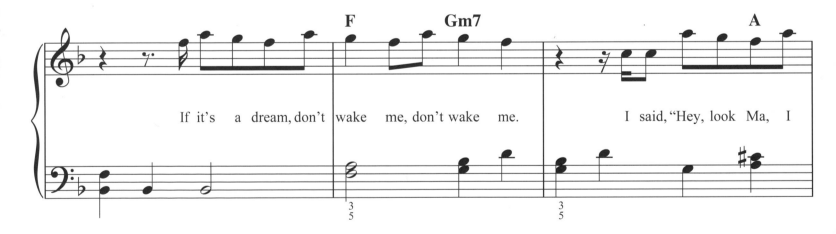

If it's a dream, don't wake me, don't wake me. I said, "Hey, look Ma, I

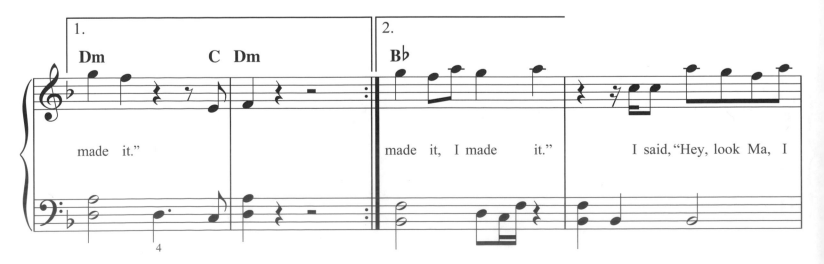

made it." made it, I made it." I said, "Hey, look Ma, I

made it, I made it."   I see it, I want it, I take it, take it.

If it's a dream, don't wake me, don't wake me.   I said, "Hey, look Ma, I

made it. (Ma-ma best be-lieve it.)   Hey, look Ma, I made it. (Think I must be dream-ing.)

1.   Hey, look Ma, I

2.   Hey, look Ma, I made it."

THE HYPE

Words and Music by PAUL MEANY
and TYLER JOSEPH

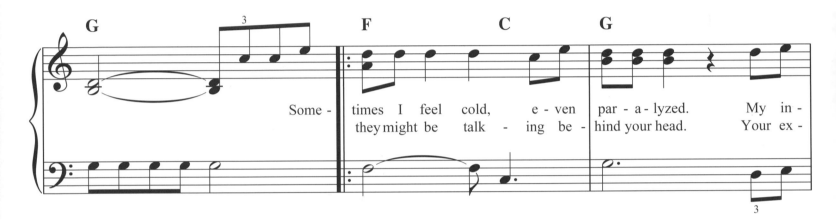

Some - times I feel cold, e - ven par - a - lyzed. My in -
they might be talk - ing be - hind your head. Your ex -

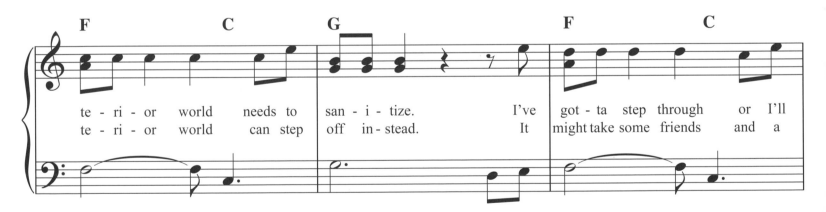

te - ri - or world needs to san - i - tize. I've got - ta step through or I'll
te - ri - or world can step off in - stead. It might take some friends and a

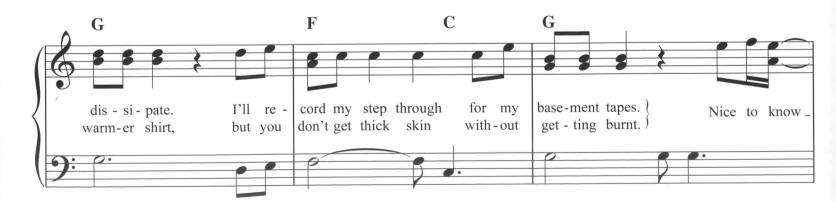

dis - si - pate. I'll re - cord my step through for my base - ment tapes. Nice to know
warm - er shirt, but you don't get thick skin with - out get - ting burnt.

Copyright © 2018 Marigny Music, Warner-Tamerlane Publishing Corp., Fueled By Music, Inc. and Stryker Joseph Music
All Rights for Marigny Music Administered Worldwide by Kobalt Songs Music Publishing
All Rights for Fueled By Music, Inc. and Stryker Joseph Music Administered by Warner-Tamerlane Publishing Corp.
All Rights Reserved   Used by Permission

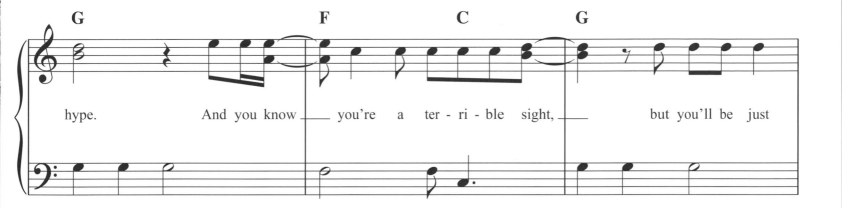

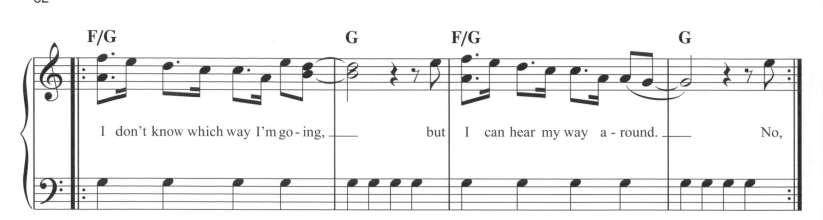

I don't know which way I'm go-ing, _____ but I can hear my way a-round. _____ No,

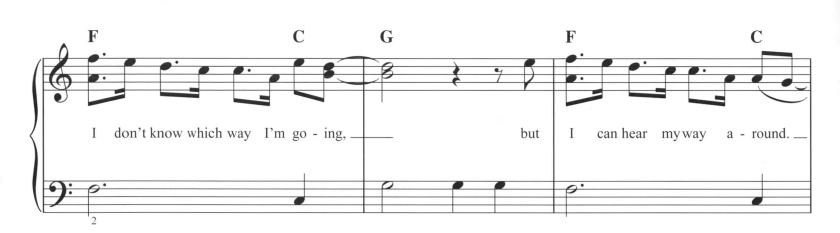

I don't know which way I'm go-ing, _____ but I can hear my way a-round. _____

_____ No, I don't know which way I'm go-ing, _____ but

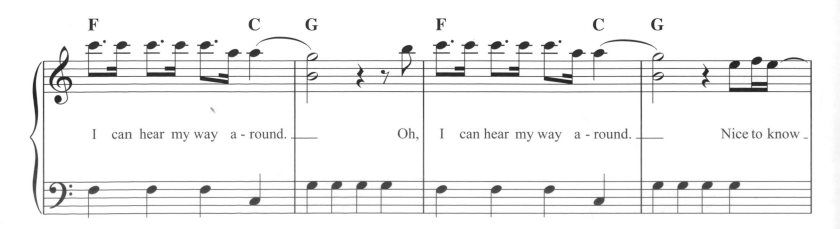

I can hear my way a-round. _____ Oh, I can hear my way a-round. _____ Nice to know _____

my _____ kind ___ will be on my side. I don't be - lieve the

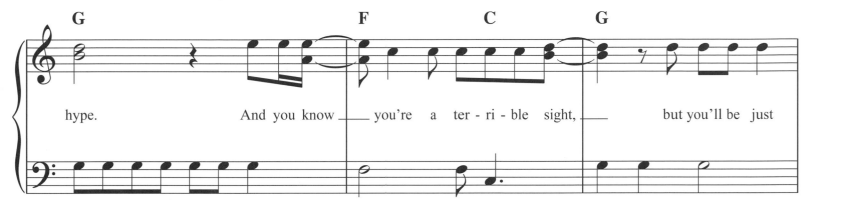

hype. And you know ____ you're a ter - ri - ble sight, ___ but you'll be just

fine. Just don't be - lieve the hype. Nice to know ____ my ____ kind _

___ will be on my side. I don't be - lieve the hype. And you know _

64

you're a ter-ri-ble sight, _ but you'll be just fine. Just don't be-lieve the

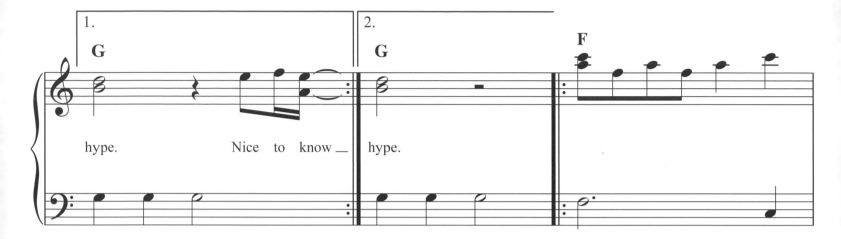

hype. Nice to know _ hype.

LIFE IN THE CITY

Words and Music by JEREMY FRAITES
and WESLEY SCHULTZ

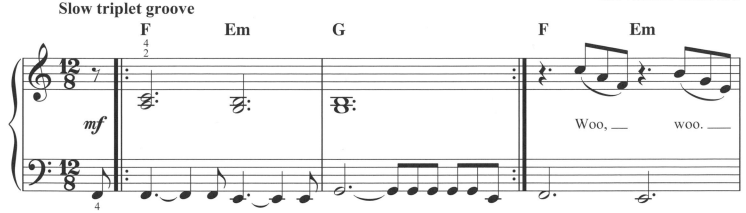

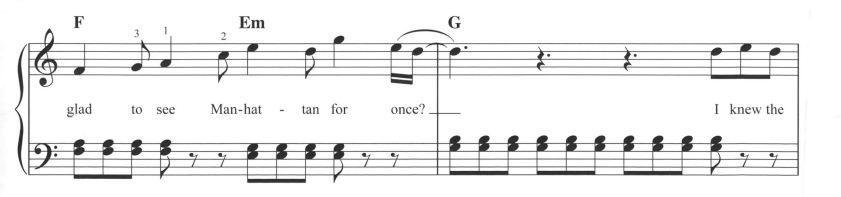

Copyright © 2019 The Lumineers
All Rights Administered Worldwide by Songs Of Kobalt Music Publishing
All Rights Reserved   Used by Permission

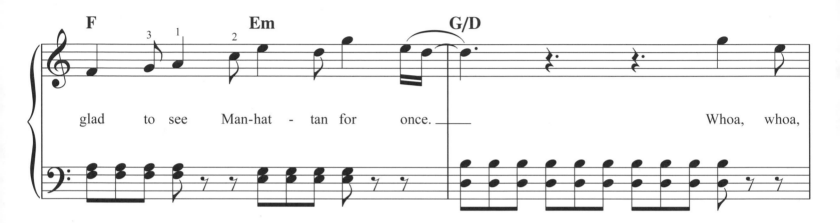

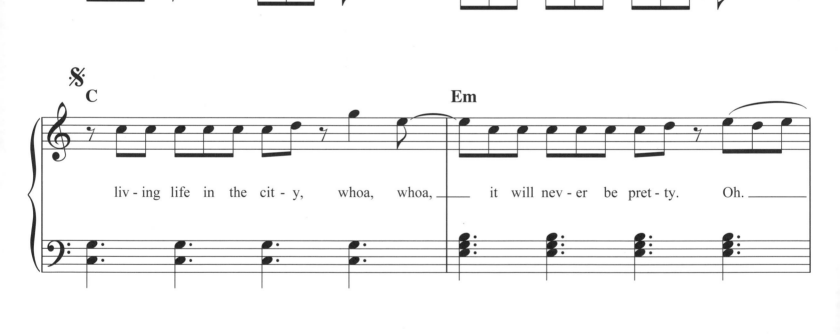

we can plan if we make it. Whoa, whoa, ___ we won't let 'em, they won't take it from me.

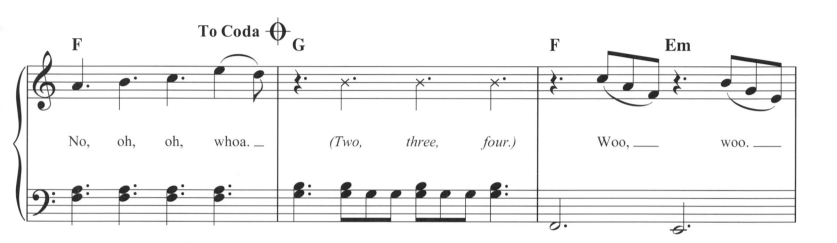

No, oh, oh, whoa. ___ *(Two, three, four.)* Woo, ___ woo. ___

Woo, ___ woo. ___ And if you

leave, ___ don't leave me all a- lone; ___ 'cause I'll be

scared, _____ I'll be na-ked, I'll be cold. And I miss my

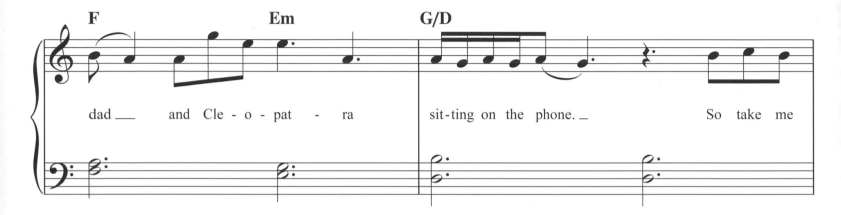

dad __ and Cle-o-pat - ra sit-ting on the phone. _ So take me

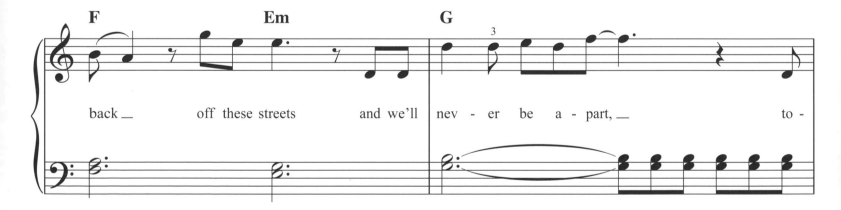

back __ off these streets and we'll nev - er be a - part, __ to-

D.S. al Coda

geth-er from the start, _ nev-er, nev-er fall - ing back a - lone. _ Whoa, _ whoa,

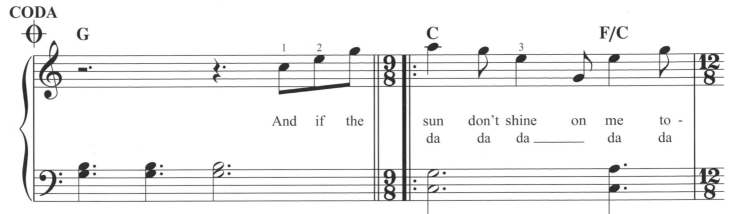

CODA

And if the sun don't shine on me to -
da da da da da da

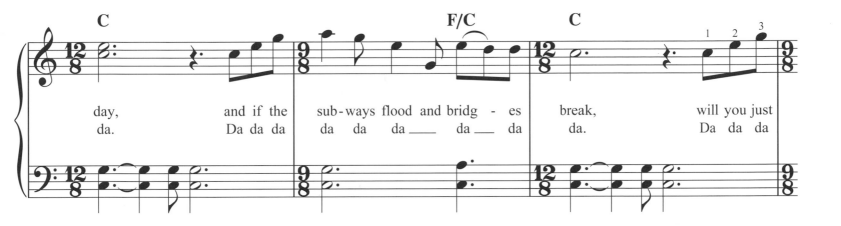

day, and if the sub-ways flood and bridg - es break, will you just
da. Da da da da da da da da da. Da da da

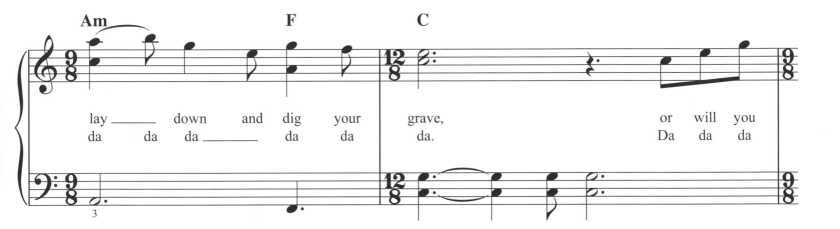

lay down and dig your grave, or will you
da da da da da da. Da da da

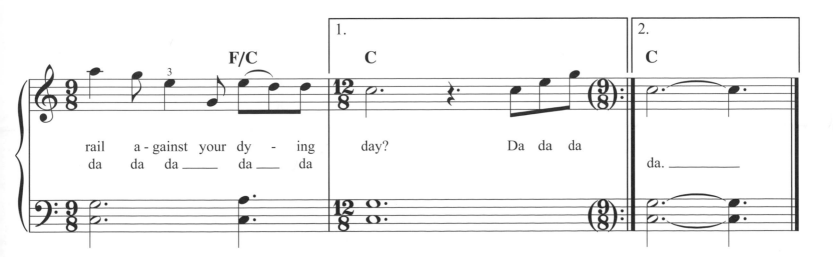

rail a-gainst your dy - ing day? Da da da
da da da da da da. da.

LOSE YOU TO LOVE ME

Words and Music by SELENA GOMEZ,
JUSTIN TRANTER, JULIA MICHAELS,
ROBIN FREDRIKSSON and MATTIAS LARSSON

Slowly, in 2

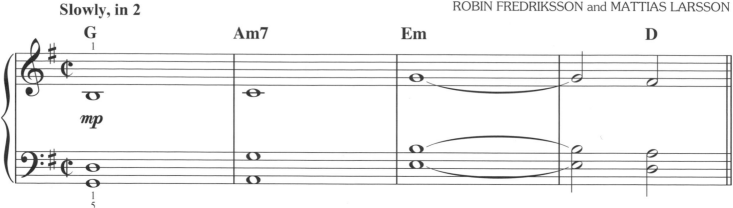

You prom-ised the world and I fell for it.
I saw the signs and I ig-nored it.

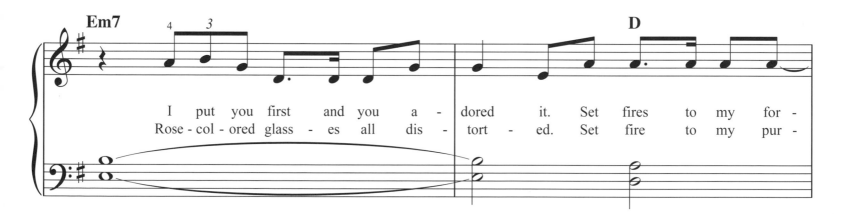

I put you first and you a-dored it. Set fires to my for-
Rose-col-ored glass-es all dis-tort-ed. Set fire to my pur-

-est, and you let it burn.
-pose, and I let it burn.

Sang off-key in my cho-
You got off on the hurt-

Copyright © 2019 UNIVERSAL MUSIC CORP., SMG TUNES, WARNER-TAMERLANE PUBLISHING CORP.,
JUSTIN'S SCHOOL FOR GIRLS, I'VE GOT ISSUES MUSIC, WC MUSIC CORP. and SONGS OF WOLF COUSINS
All Rights for SMG TUNES Administered by UNIVERSAL MUSIC CORP.
All Rights for JUSTIN'S SCHOOL FOR GIRLS and I'VE GOT ISSUES MUSIC Administered by WARNER-TAMERLANE PUBLISHING CORP.
All Rights for SONGS OF WOLF COUSINS Administered by WC MUSIC CORP.
All Rights Reserved   Used by Permission

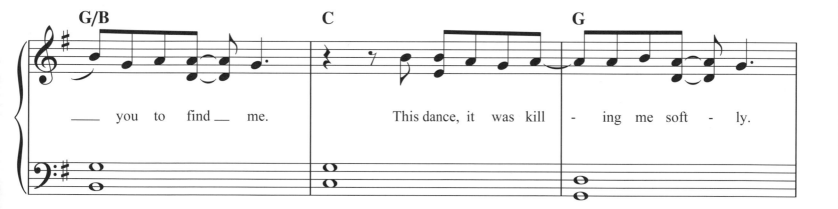

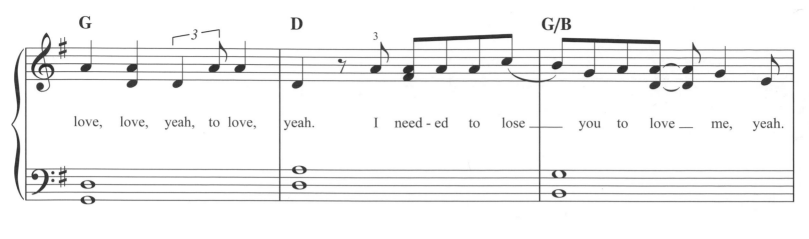

us like it was eas - y. Made me think I de - served

it in the thick of heal - ing, yeah.

You prom - ised the world and I fell for it.

I put you first and you a - dored it. Set fires to my for -

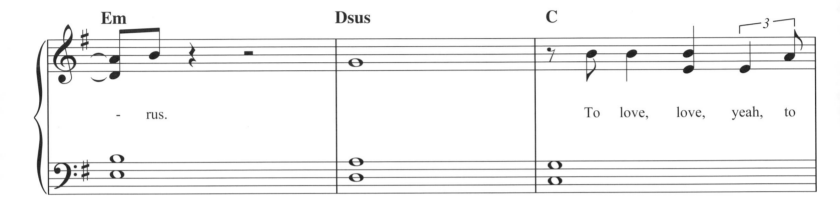

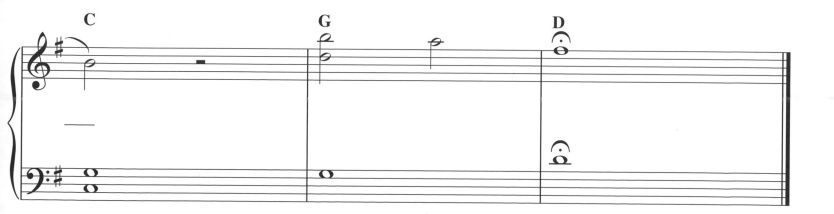

LOVER

Words and Music by
TAYLOR SWIFT

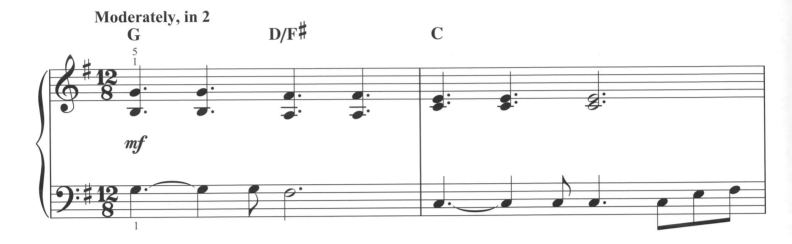

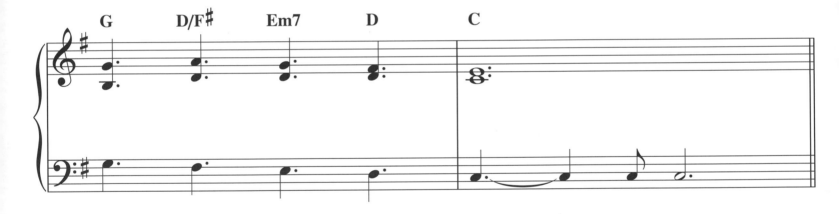

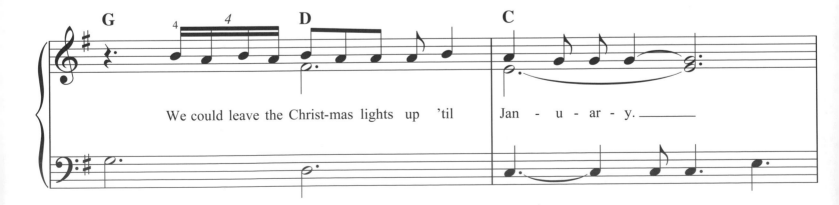

Copyright © 2019 Sony/ATV Music Publishing LLC and Taylor Swift Music
All Rights Administered by Sony/ATV Music Publishing LLC, 424 Church Street, Suite 1200, Nashville, TN 37219
International Copyright Secured   All Rights Reserved

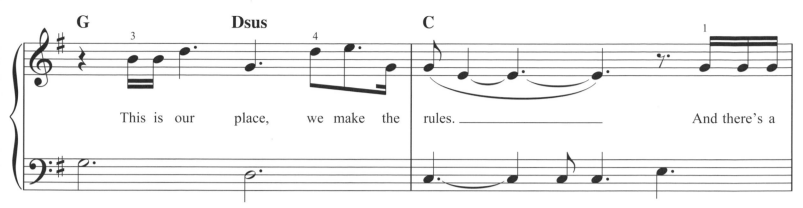

This is our place, we make the rules. _____ And there's a

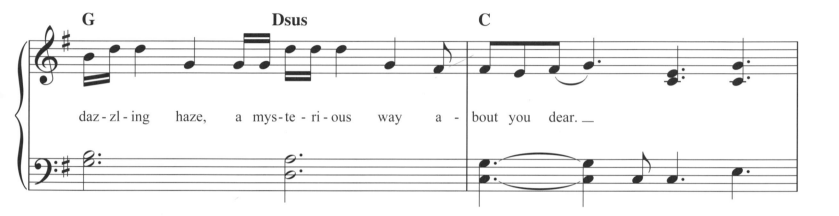

daz - zl - ing haze, a mys - te - ri - ous way a - bout you dear. __

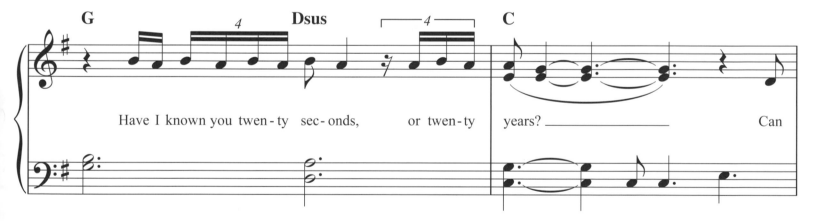

Have I known you twen - ty sec - onds, or twen - ty years? _____ Can

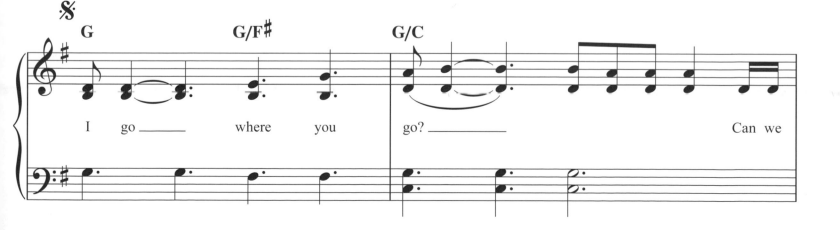

I go _____ where you go? _____ Can we

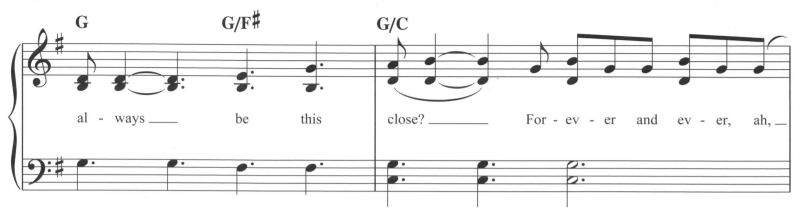

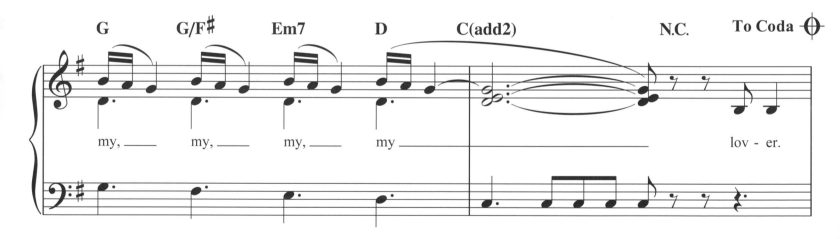

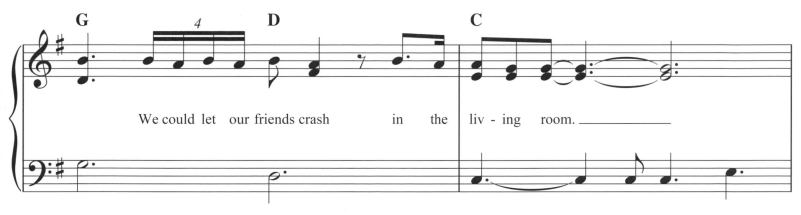

We could let our friends crash in the liv-ing room. ____

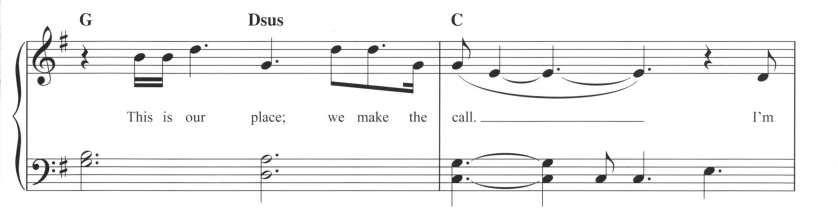

This is our place; we make the call. ____ I'm

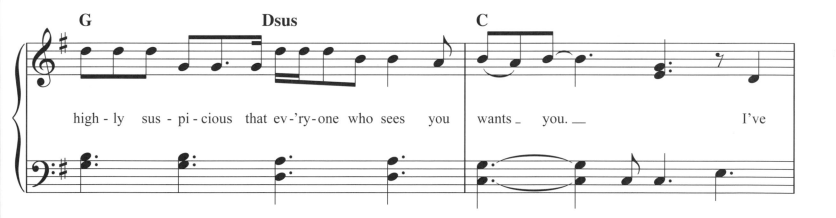

high-ly sus-pi-cious that ev-'ry-one who sees you wants _ you. __ I've

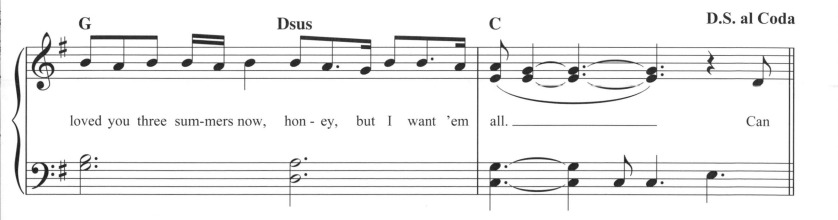

loved you three sum-mers now, hon-ey, but I want 'em all. ____ Can

CODA

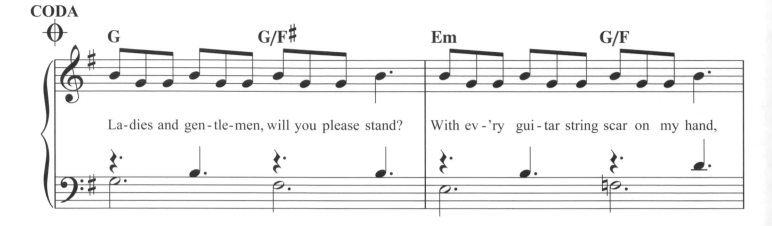

G   G/F#   Em   G/F

La-dies and gen-tle-men, will you please stand?   With ev-'ry gui-tar string scar on my hand,

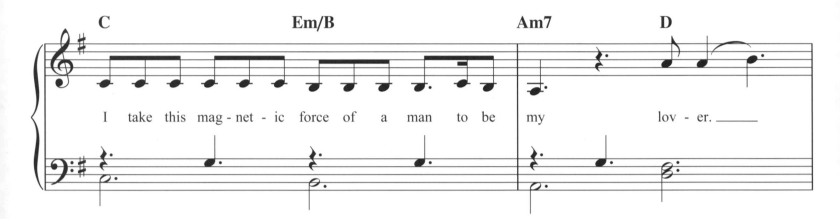

C   Em/B   Am7   D

I take this mag-net-ic force of a man to be my lov-er. _____

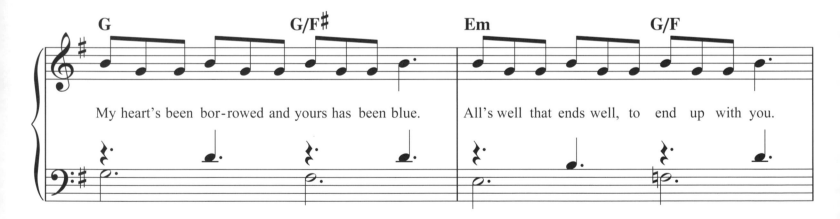

G   G/F#   Em   G/F

My heart's been bor-rowed and yours has been blue.   All's well that ends well, to end up with you.

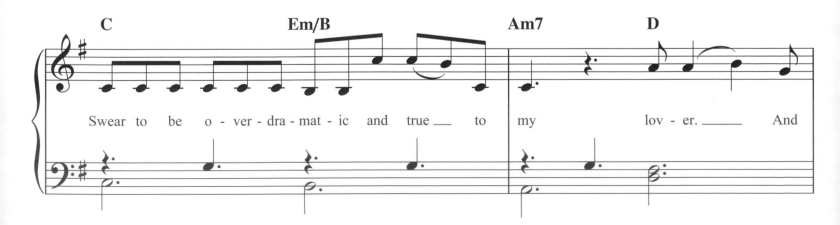

C   Em/B   Am7   D

Swear to be o-ver-dra-mat-ic and true _____ to my lov-er. _____ And

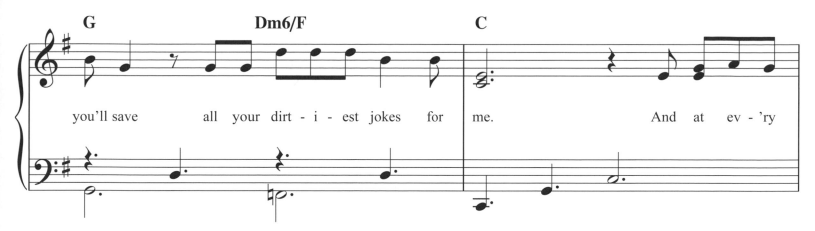

you'll save all your dirt - i - est jokes for me. And at ev - 'ry

ta - ble _____ I'll save you a seat, lov - er. ____ Can

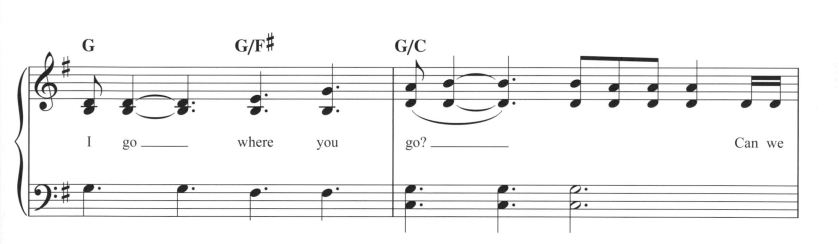

I go ____ where you go? _____ Can we

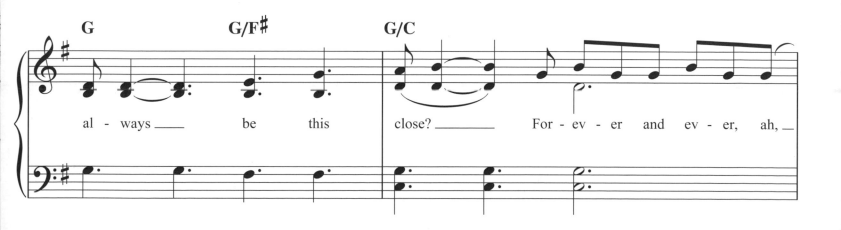

al - ways ____ be this close? _____ For - ev - er and ev - er, ah, ___

take me out and take me home. _____ You're

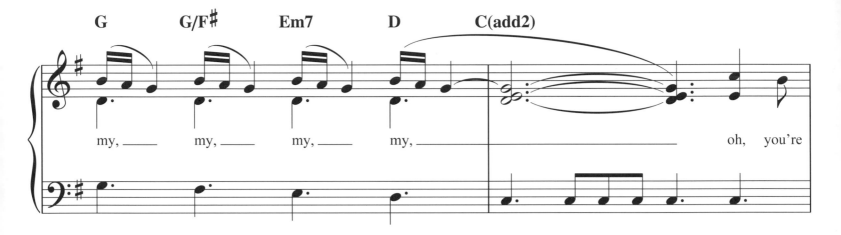

my, _____ my, _____ my, _____ my, _____ oh, you're

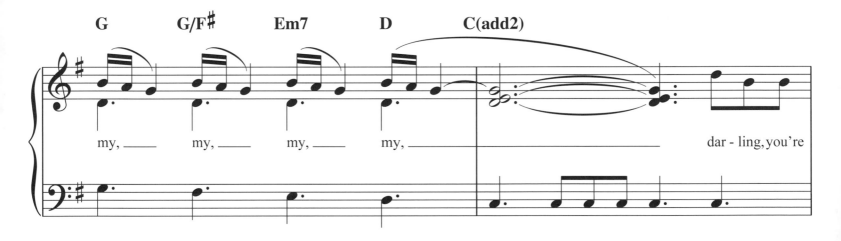

my, _____ my, _____ my, _____ my, _____ dar - ling, you're

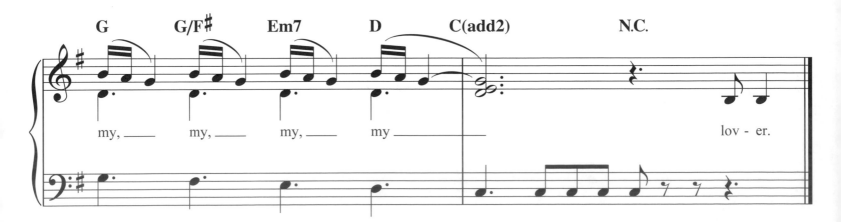

my, _____ my, _____ my, _____ my lov - er.

TRUTH HURTS

Words and Music by LIZZO,
ERIC FREDERIC, JESSE ST. JOHN GELLER
and STEVEN CHEUNG

Moderately, in 2

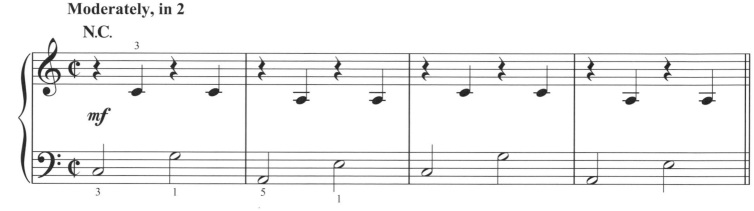

Why men great 'til they got-ta be great? *Woo!*

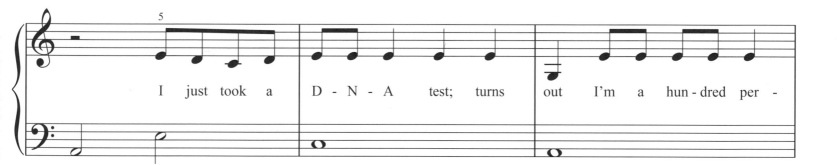

I just took a D-N-A test; turns out I'm a hun-dred per-

cent that kid e-ven when I'm cry-in' cra-zy. Yeah, I got boy prob-lems, that's the

© 2019 WARNER-TAMERLANE PUBLISHING CORP., MELISSA JEFFERSON PUBLISHING DESIGNEE, SONY/ATV MUSIC PUBLISHING LLC,
EMI BLACKWOOD MUSIC INC., SONGS FROM THE BOARDWALK, FREDERIC AND RIED MUSIC,
JESSE SJ MUSIC, BIG DEAL NOTES, TELE THE BUSINESS and ALVARADO AND SUNSET MUSIC
All Rights for MELISSA JEFFERSON PUBLISHING DESIGNEE Administered by WARNER-TAMERLANE PUBLISHING CORP.
All Rights for SONY/ATV MUSIC PUBLISHING LLC, EMI BLACKWOOD MUSIC INC., SONGS FROM THE BOARDWALK, FREDERIC AND RIED MUSIC
and JESSE SJ MUSIC Administered by SONY/ATV MUSIC PUBLISHING LLC, 424 Church Street, Suite 1200, Nashville, TN 37219
All Rights for BIG DEAL NOTES, TELE THE BUSINESS and ALVARADO AND SUNSET MUSIC Administered by WORDS & MUSIC, a division of BIG DEAL MUSIC GROUP
All Rights Reserved   Used by Permission

hu - man in me. ___ Bling, bling, then I solve 'em, that's the god-dess in me. You could - a had a

good friend, non - com - mit - tal. Help you with your ca - reer just a

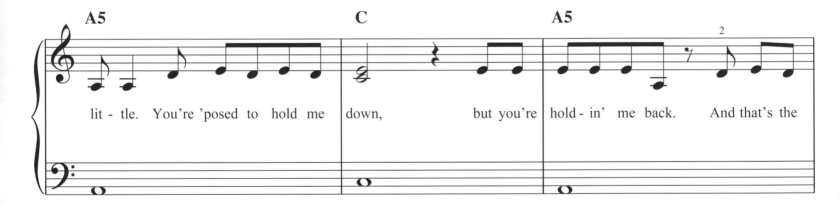

lit - tle. You're 'posed to hold me down, but you're hold - in' me back. And that's the

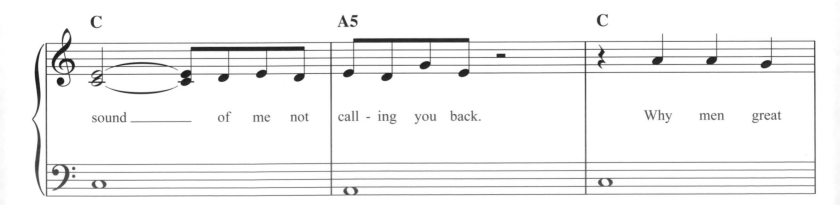

sound ___ of me not call - ing you back. Why men great

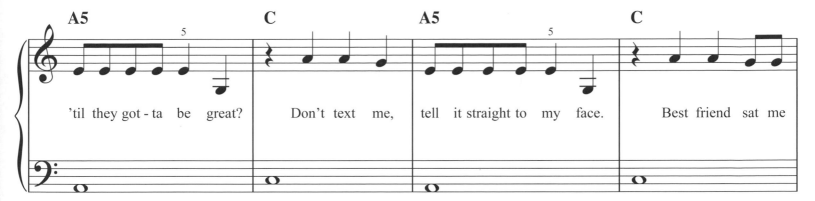

'til they got-ta be great? | Don't text me, tell it straight to my face. | Best friend sat me

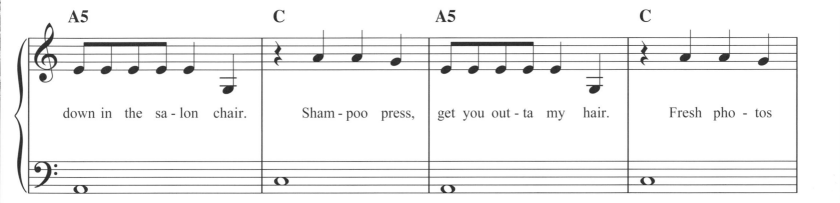

down in the sa-lon chair. | Sham-poo press, get you out-ta my hair. | Fresh pho-tos

with the bon light-ing. | New man on the Min-ne-so-ta Vi-kings. | Truth hurts, need-ed

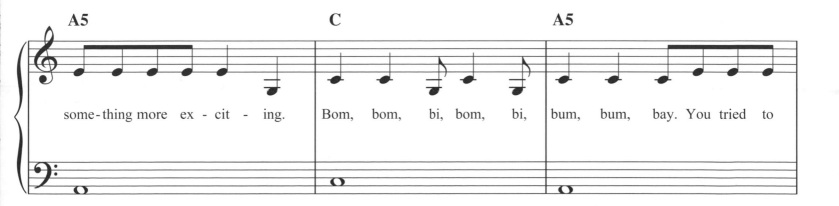

some-thing more ex-cit-ing. | Bom, bom, bi, bom, bi, bum, bum, bay. You tried to

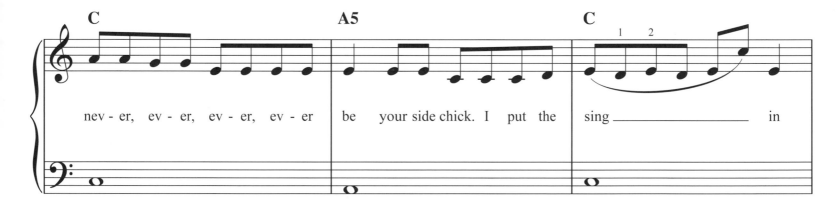

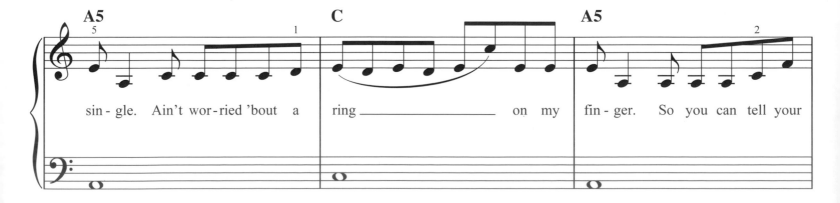

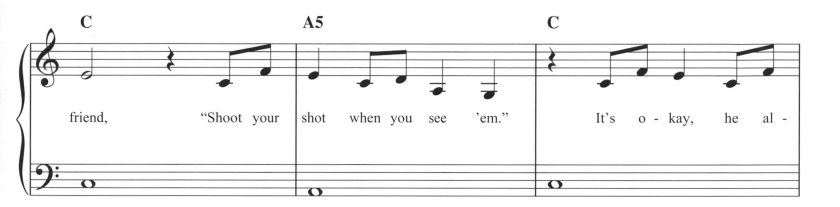

friend, "Shoot your shot when you see 'em." It's o - kay, he al -

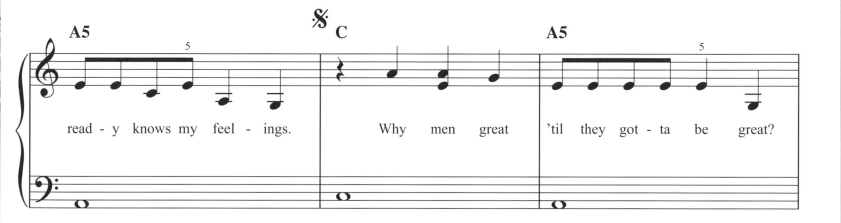

read - y knows my feel - ings. Why men great 'til they got - ta be great?

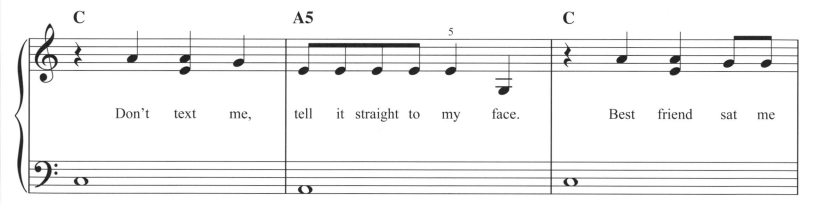

Don't text me, tell it straight to my face. Best friend sat me

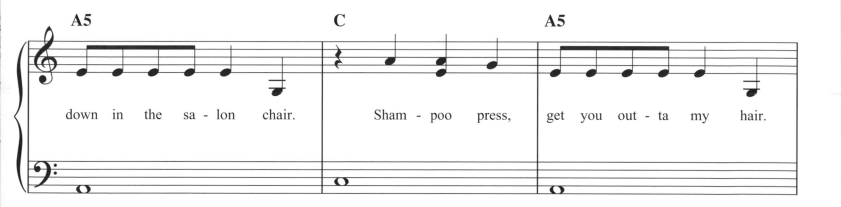

down in the sa - lon chair. Sham - poo press, get you out - ta my hair.

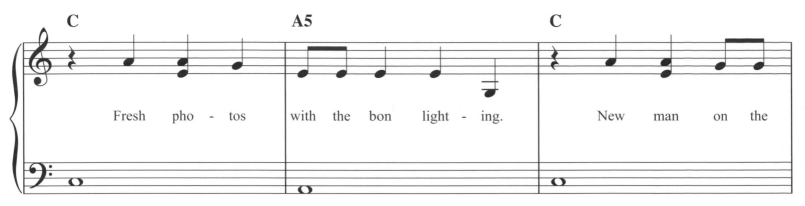

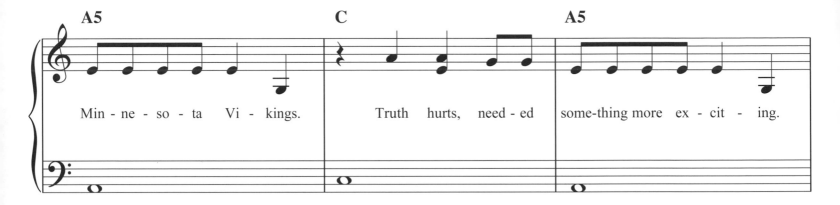

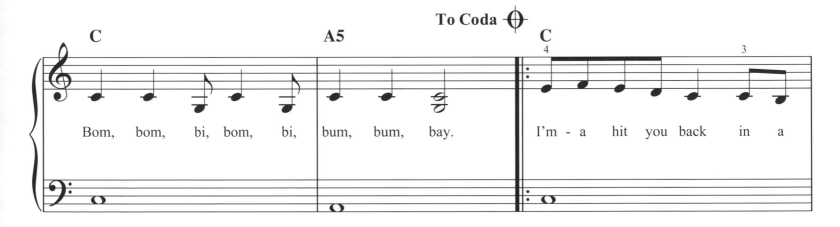

We don't deal with lies, we don't do good-byes. We just keep it push-in' like

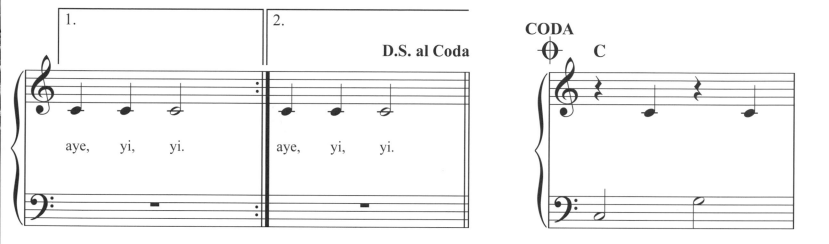

1. aye, yi, yi.

2. aye, yi, yi.

D.S. al Coda

CODA

With the bomb light-ing. Min-ne-so-ta

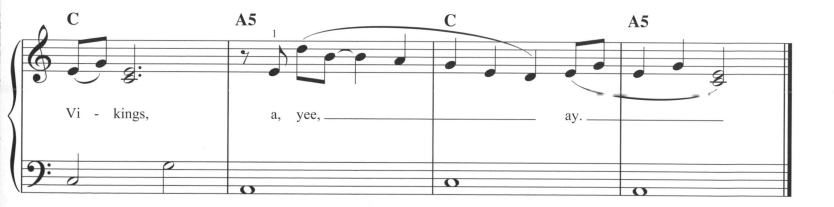

Vi-kings, a, yee, ay.

MEMORIES

Words and Music by ADEM LEVINE,
JONATHAN BELLION, JORDAN JOHNSON,
JACOB HINDLIN, STEFAN JOHNSON,
MICHAEL POLLACK and VINCENT FORD

Relaxed groove

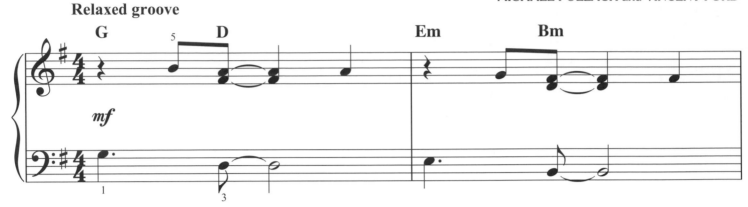

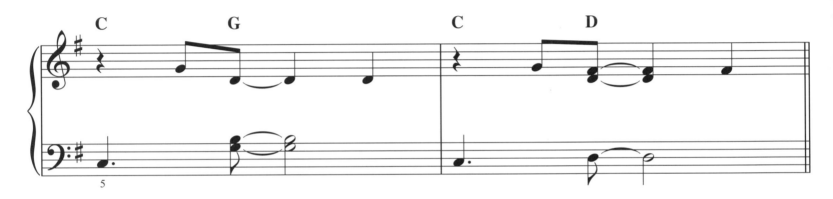

Here's to the ones that we got, cheers to the wish you were here, but you're not. 'Cause the

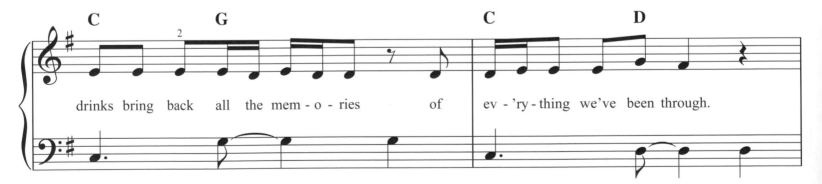

drinks bring back all the mem-o-ries of ev-'ry-thing we've been through.

Copyright © 2019 Sudgee 2 Music, Songs Of Universal, Inc., Art In The Fodder Music, BMG Bumblebee, Songs Of A Beautiful Mind, BMG Platinum Songs US,
R8D Music, Songs Of BBMG, Rap Kingpin Music, Prescription Songs, 1916 Publishing, Warner-Tamerlane Publishing Corp.,
What Key Do You Want It In Music, Songs With A Pure Tone, Fifty-Six Hope Road Music Ltd. and Primary Wave/Blue Mountain
All Rights for Sudgee 2 Music and Art In The Fodder Music Administered by Songs Of Universal, Inc.
All Rights for BMG Bumblebee, Songs Of A Beautiful Mind, BMG Platinum Songs US, R8D Music and Songs Of BBMG Administered by BMG Rights Management (US) LLC
All Rights for Rap Kingpin Music, Prescription Songs and 1916 Publishing Administered Worldwide by Kobalt Songs Music Publishing
All Rights for What Key Do You Want It In Music and Songs With A Pure Tone Administered by Warner-Tamerlane Publishing Corp.
All Rights for Fifty-Six Hope Road Music Ltd. and Primary Wave/Blue Mountain Administered in North America
by Blue Mountain Music Ltd./Irish Town Songs and throughout the rest of the world by Blue Mountain Music Ltd.
All Rights Reserved   Used by Permission

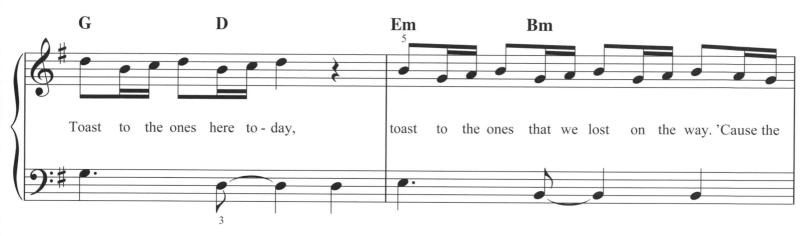

Toast to the ones here to-day, toast to the ones that we lost on the way. 'Cause the

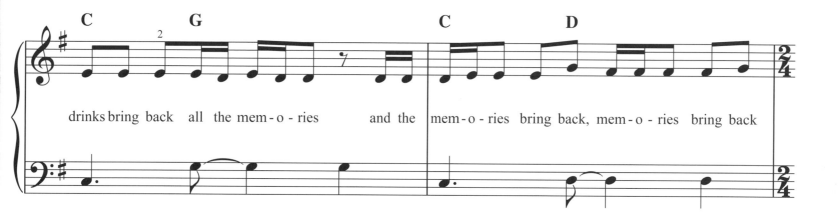

drinks bring back all the mem-o-ries and the mem-o-ries bring back, mem-o-ries bring back

you. There's a time that I ___ re-mem-ber when I
time that I ___ re-mem-ber when I

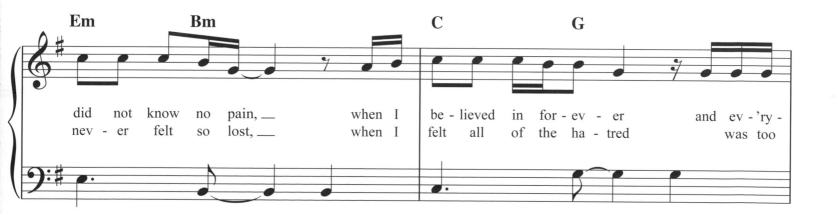

did not know no pain, ___ when I be-lieved in for-ev-er and ev-'ry-
nev-er felt so lost, ___ when I felt all of the ha-tred was too

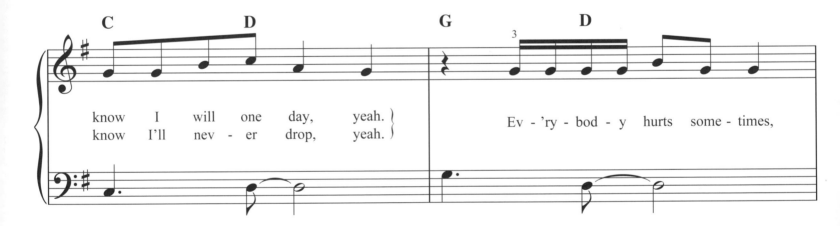

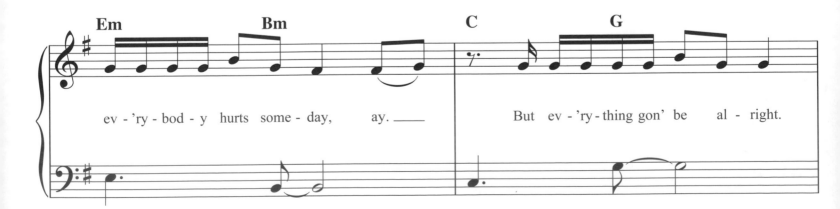

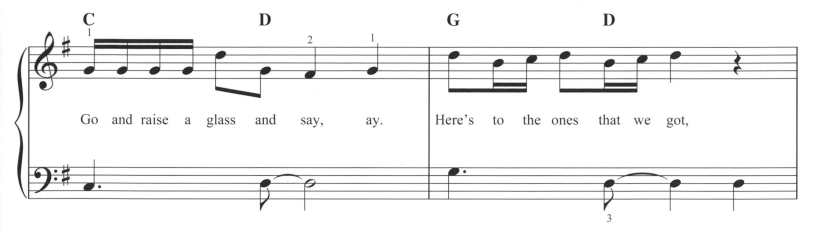

Go and raise a glass and say, ay. Here's to the ones that we got,

cheers to the wish you were here, but you're not. 'Cause the drinks bring back all the mem-o-ries of

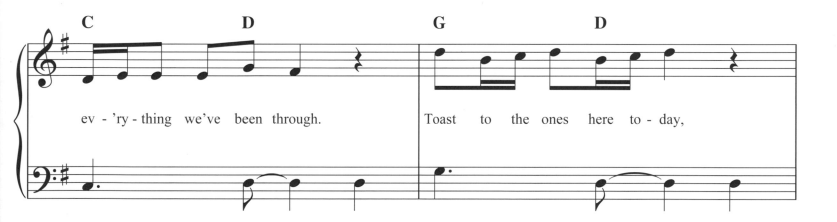

ev-'ry-thing we've been through. Toast to the ones here to-day,

toast to the ones that we lost on the way. 'Cause the drinks bring back all the mem-o-ries and the

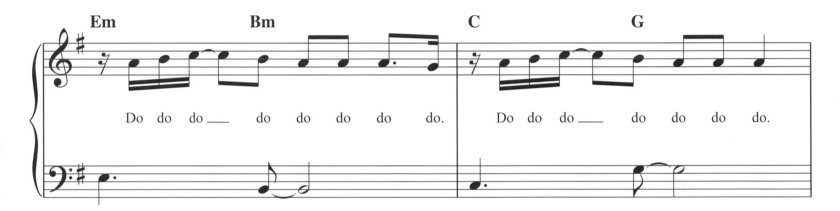

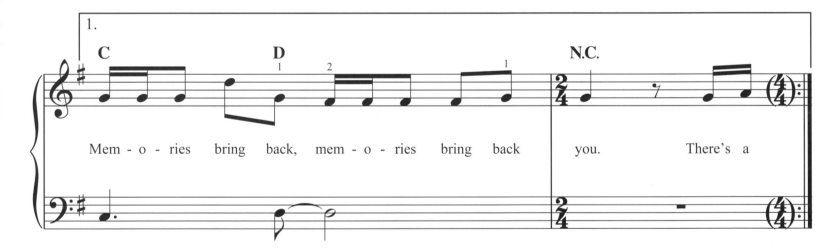

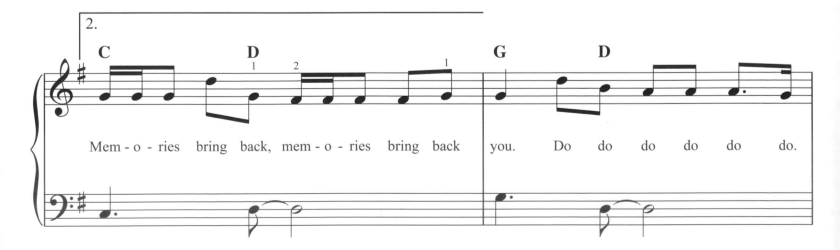

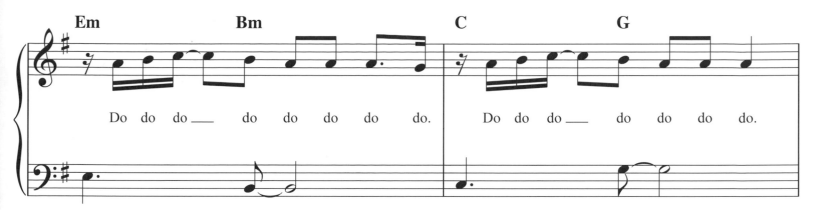

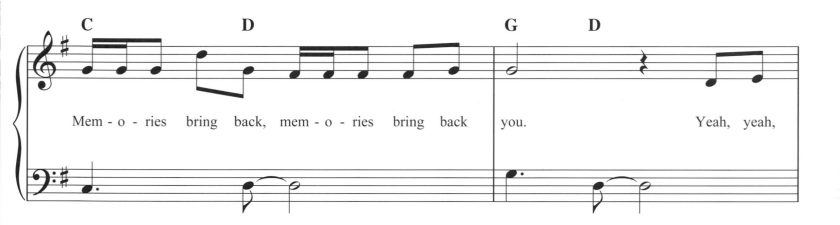

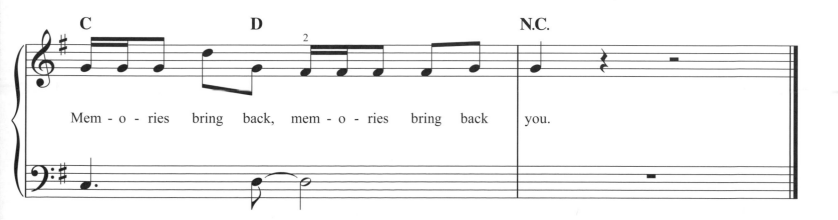

10,000 HOURS

Words and Music by DAN SMYERS,
JORDAN REYNOLDS, SHAY MOONEY,
JUSTIN BIEBER, JASON BOYD
and JESSIE JO DILLON

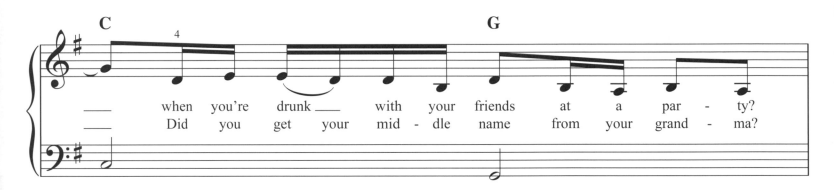

© 2019 WC MUSIC CORP., BEATS AND BANJOS, BUCKEYE26, JREYNMUSIC, WARNER-TAMERLANE PUBLISHING CORP., SHAY MOONEY MUSIC,
UNIVERSAL MUSIC CORP., BIEBER TIME PUBLISHING, BMG GOLD SONGS, POO BZ PUBLISHING INC., BIG MUSIC MACHINE and BIG ASS PILE OF DIMES MUSIC
All Rights for BEATS AND BANJOS, BUCKEYE26 and JREYNMUSIC Administered by WC MUSIC CORP.
All Rights for SHAY MOONEY MUSIC Administered by WARNER-TAMERLANE PUBLISHING CORP.
All Rights for BIEBER TIME PUBLISHING Administered by UNIVERSAL MUSIC CORP.
All Rights for BMG GOLD SONGS and POO BZ PUBLISHING INC. Administered by BMG RIGHTS MANAGEMENT (US) LLC
All Rights Reserved   Used by Permission

98

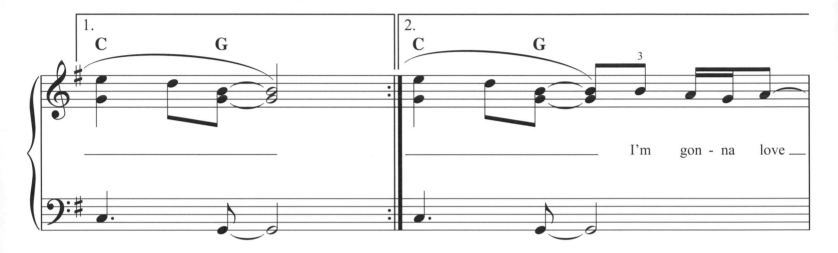

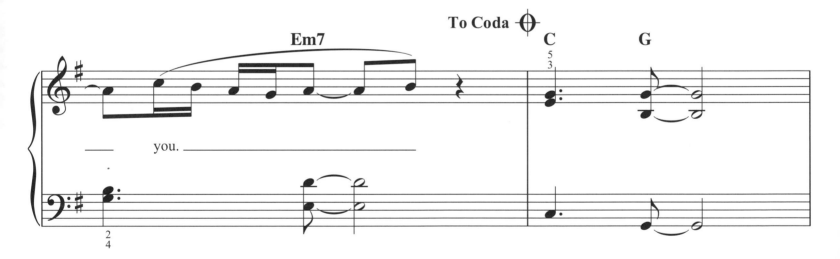

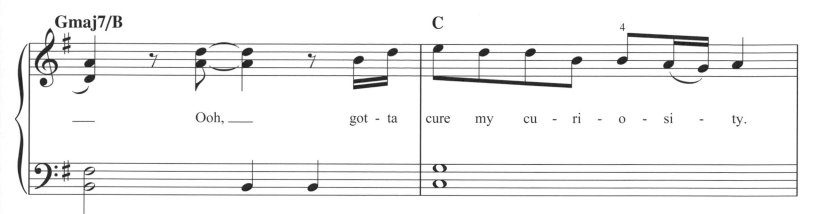

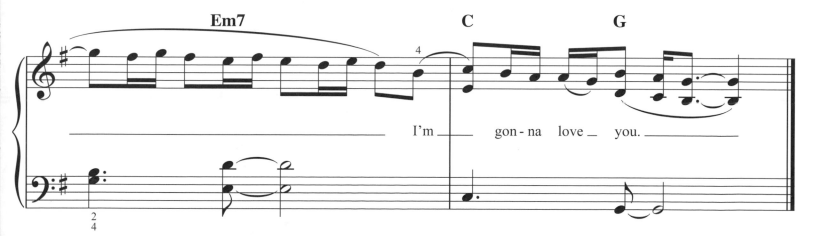

ONLY HUMAN

Words and Music by NICK JONAS,
JOSEPH JONAS, SHELLBACK
and KEVIN JONAS

Moderate Reggae

I don't want this night to end. It's clos-

-in' time __ so leave __ with me __ a - gain, __ yeah. __

Copyright © 2019 SONGS OF UNIVERSAL, INC., NICK JONAS PUBLISHING, JOSEPH JONAS PUBLISHING, MXM and KEVIN JONAS PUBLISHING DESIGNEE
All Rights for NICK JONAS PUBLISHING and JOSEPH JONAS PUBLISHING Administered by SONGS OF UNIVERSAL, INC.
All Rights for MXM Administered Worldwide by KOBALT SONGS MUSIC PUBLISHING
All Rights Reserved   Used by Permission

You got all my love to spend. ___ Oh, let's find

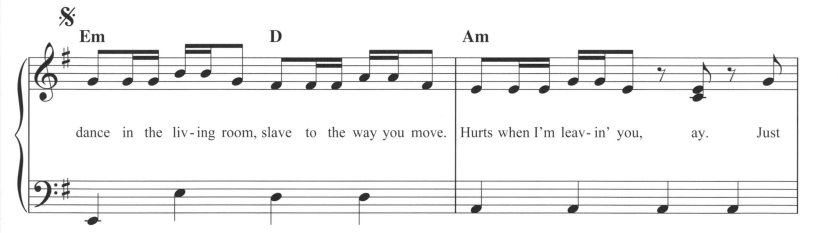

___ a place ___ where hap - pi - ness ___ be - gins. ___ We gon'

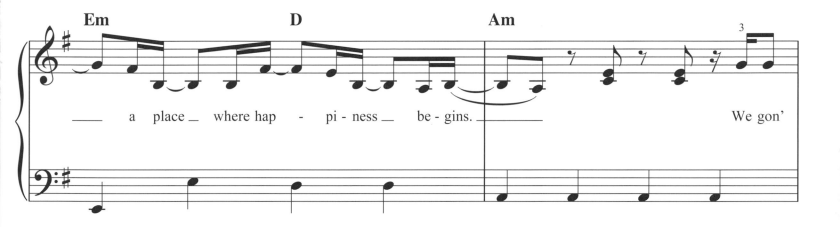

dance in the liv-ing room, slave to the way you move. Hurts when I'm leav- in' you, ay. Just

dance in the liv-ing room, love with an at - ti - tude. Drunk to an eight - ies groove, ___ ay. We gon'

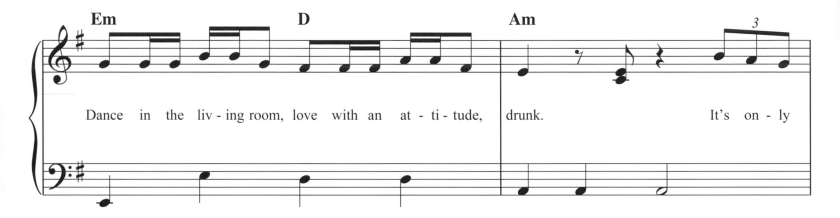

stop pre-tend-ing you're shy, just come on and dance, dance, dance, dance,

oh.

Ear - ly morn - in' la - la - light. On -

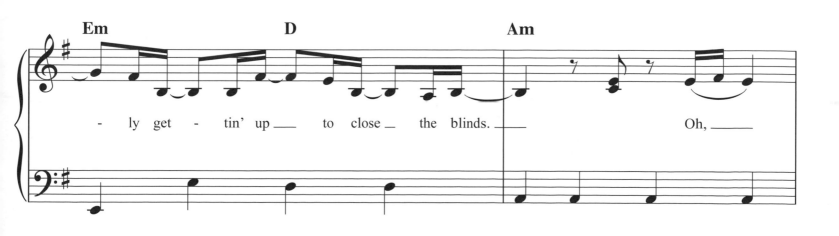

- ly get - tin' up to close the blinds. Oh,

I'm pray-ing you don't change your mind ___ 'cause leav-in' now just don't feel right. ___

D.S. al Coda

___ Let's do it one ___ more time. _____ We gon'

CODA

oh.

On - ly hu -

man. It's on-ly man, it's on-ly man, on-ly hu - man.